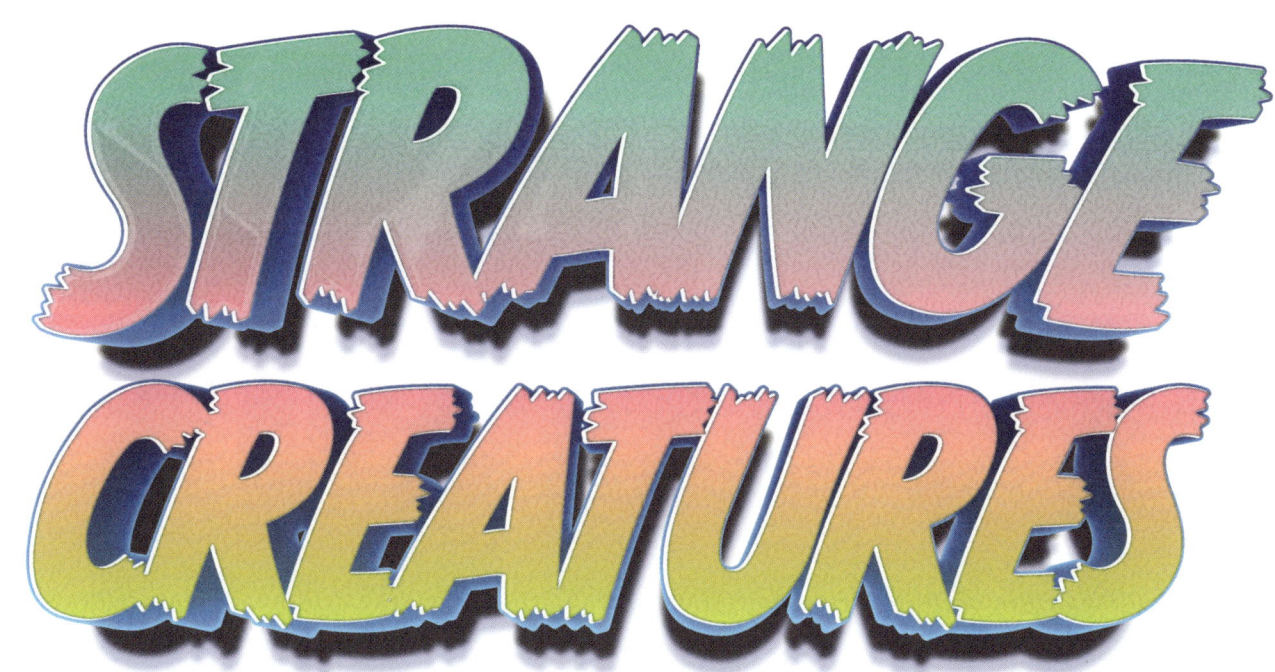

EXPLORING THE WONDERFUL AND WEIRD ANIMALS THAT SHARE THIS PLANET WITH US

WRITTEN BY DYLAN DUBEAU AND ANDRES SALAZAR

EDITED BY ANDRES SALAZAR

CORAL GABLES

Copyright © 2024 by Blue Ant Media Digital Inc.

Published by Mango Publishing, a division of Mango Publishing Group, Inc.

Cover & Layout Design: Megan Werner
Cover & Interior Photos: adobe.stock.com
Illustrations: Danielle Dufault

Mango is an active supporter of authors' rights to free speech and artistic expression in their books. The purpose of copyright is to encourage authors to produce exceptional works that enrich our culture and our open society. Uploading or distributing photos, scans or any content from this book without prior permission is theft of the author's intellectual property. Please honor the author's work as you would your own. Thank you in advance for respecting our author's rights.

For permission requests, please contact the publisher at:
Mango Publishing Group
5966 South Dixie Highway, Suite 300
Miami, FL 33143 USA
info@mango.bz

For special orders, quantity sales, course adoptions and corporate sales, please email the publisher at sales@mango.bz. For trade and wholesale sales, please contact Ingram Publisher Services at customer.service@ingramcontent.com or +1.800.509.4887.

Strange Creatures: Exploring the Wonderful and Weird Animals that Share This Planet with Us

Library of Congress Cataloging-in-Publication number: 2024940107
ISBN: (p) 978-1-68481-647-7 (e) 978-1-68481-648-4
BISAC category code: JNF003000, JUVENILE NONFICTION / Animals / General

contributing authors: Emily Richardson, Lauren Greenwood, Kristen Watt

CONTENTS

Introduction	6
Chapter 1: Manta Ray	8
Chapter 2: Secretary Bird	14
Chapter 3: Snapping Turtles	19
Chapter 4: Frogfishes	24
Chapter 5: Basking Shark	29
Chapter 6: Chimaeras	34
Chapter 7: Weaver Ants	38
Chapter 8: Millipedes	43
Chapter 9: Diving Beetles	48
Chapter 10: Gharial	53
Chapter 11: Coconut Crab	58
Chapter 12: Condors	63
Chapter 13: Pallas's Cat	68
Chapter 14: Echidnas	73
Chapter 15: Tawny Frogmouths	79
Chapter 16: Wombats	83
Chapter 17: Bandicoots	89
Chapter 18: Platypus	93
Chapter 19: Hognoses	100
Chapter 20: Glow Worms	105
Chapter 21: Elephant and Harbour Seals	109
Chapter 22: Japanese Spider Crab	115
Chapter 23: Banana Slugs	120
Chapter 24: Mudskippers	125
Chapter 25: Colugos	131
Chapter 26: Raccoon Dogs	136
Chapter 27: Porcupines	142
Chapter 28: Saigas	148
Chapter 29: Velvet Worms	153
Chapter 30: Wolf Eel	158
Chapter 31: Bush Dog	163
Chapter 32: Chevrotains	168
Chapter 33: Red-Lipped Batfish	173
Chapter 34: South American River Dolphins	179
Chapter 35: Capybara	185
Chapter 36: Stargazers	190
Chapter 37: Garter Snakes	195
Chapter 38: Japanese Macaques	201
Chapter 39: Siberian Musk Deer	207
Chapter 40: Pangolins	212
Chapter 41: Tibetan Fox	217
Chapter 42: Bear Cuscuses	222
Chapter 43: Prairie Dogs	227
Conclusion	233
About Animalogic	234

Introduction

Thank you for picking up this book, your support means everything to us. Over the last ten years at *Animalogic*, we've researched and learned so much about the creatures of the world, and each animal surprised us in ways I didn't think possible. The more we learned, the more we wanted to not just share, but also cherish and protect. We're thrilled to bring you a little more about some of our favorites.

Some of the animals you'll read about are notorious weirdos, like the coconut crab, the frogmouth, and the magical glow worm. They're creatures that have developed incredibly unique and striking adaptations to survive in their environments. On the other hand, some of the most interesting animals look so unassuming at first glance. That is, until you pay attention long enough to watch their surprising and utterly perplexing behaviors and eccentricities unfold. Even the common house sparrow is full of surprises. I could write a soap opera about my backyard!

Last summer we were filming butcherbirds in the grasslands between Saskatchewan and Montana. Throughout the shoot, we were surrounded by prairie dog colonies. They were adorable. Their varied barks and chirps were the constant soundtrack of the prairie, and in those calls, they seemed to encode messages about each of our movements. I still wonder what gossip they were spreading about us.

We interviewed a couple of experts about them and were shocked to find out that these humble rodents were one of the most amazing animals we'd ever encountered. We learned that they not only have one of the most advanced animal languages in the world, but also live in vast underground cities larger than most human-built cities. What's more is that all of the animals in their ecosystem rely on them and their tunnels to thrive. They were right in front of us all along, and we just needed to dig a little deeper to learn how incredible they were.

That is the ethos of *Animalogic*. The world is full of wonders, and every animal can be wonderful if you take the time to watch, listen, and learn about how each creature lives and creatively adapts to a world that is constantly changing.

This book is ten years in the making. Executive producer and director Dylan Dubeau has led the team from the start, making sure every episode looks beautiful and brings something meaningful to our viewers. Producer and researcher Andres Salazar has been with us for the past five years and has helped us delve deeper into the science behind the animals we love.

We are all very proud of our work and hope to continue to share our love and appreciation of the animal world with everyone through this book.

The subjects of this book are chosen for two reasons. The first and main one is that they subvert our expectations of how animals like them should look or behave. We have a fish that walks on four "legs," a scuba diving beetle, a spiky mammal that lays leathery snake-like eggs, snakes that come out yearly for one of the largest mating events on Earth, and many more.

The second criterion is the quality of my illustrations of all these animals. Of course, they're all drawn in *Animalogic's* iconic style and they are some of my favorite illustrations I've ever drawn. But let's be honest, the longer I've been making these, the better they get!

Each chapter of the book introduces one of these animals. We'll learn about its biology, behavior, and ecology, placing a special emphasis on what makes them unique.

These are just some of our favorite stories in evolutionary biology. We hope you join us in loving these animals for all their weirdness and beauty, in appreciating the grandeur of all the nature that surrounds us, and in finding deep wonder about the beings of our planet.

Danielle Dufault

Chapter 1
Manta Ray

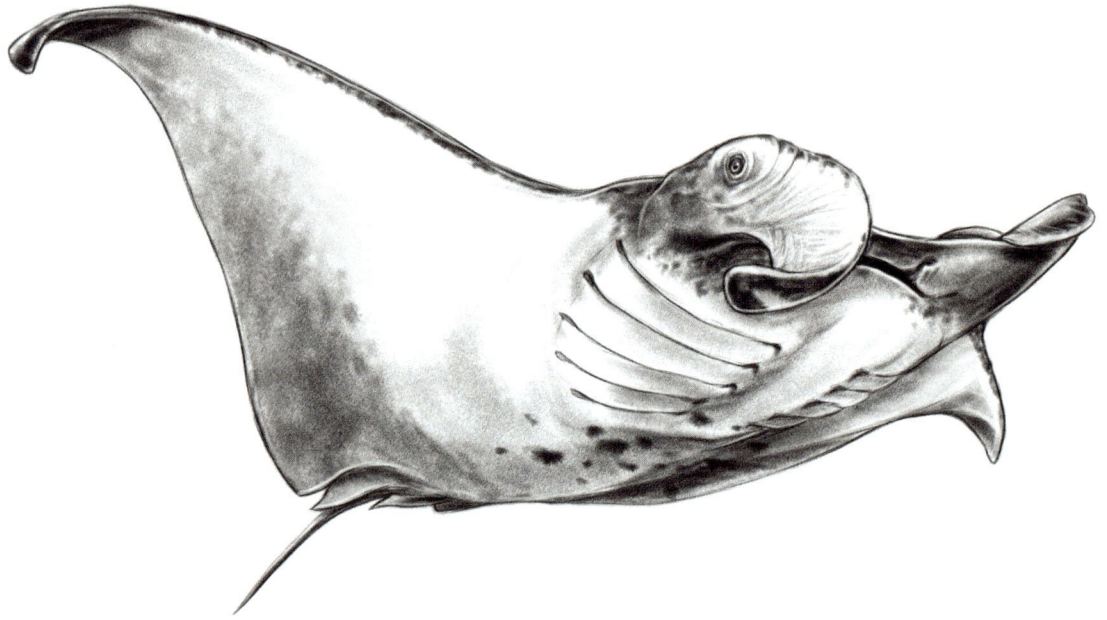

Manta rays are a fantastical-looking enormous fish with an alien appearance that has inspired countless works of science fiction. They can be up to seven meters (twenty-three feet) wide and are some of the most magical and majestic creatures in the ocean.

Rays are part of the cartilaginous fish class, along with sharks, skates, and chimaeras. They're flat sharks and have a surprisingly similar biology to their feared cousins. But what sets mantas apart from other rays is their sheer size.

An average full-grown giant manta ray is about seven meters wide, but some get even larger. The record for the largest wingspan is 9.1 meters across. That's about the same size as two elephants stacked together. At this size they're big enough to intimidate most predators. They only have to worry about some sharks, orcas, and, of course, humans.

There are two manta ray species: the reef manta ray and the giant oceanic manta ray. They belong to the genus *Mobula* and are found all over the world in warm and temperate waters.

Both species are huge and similar. The easiest way to tell them apart is by the giant manta ray's caudal spine. This is a vestigial organ, an evolutionary remnant of a once powerful sting barb, which they used to protect themselves from

predators earlier in their evolutionary history, when they were likely much smaller. But as they grew increasingly larger, the predators became rarer, and the sting barb fell out of use. In the reef manta, it has disappeared completely.

Another way to tell them apart is their habitat. Reef mantas prefer to stick closer to the coast, while giant mantas prefer the open ocean. Mantas can be seen close to the surface, but they become more common at around ten meters (thirty feet) of depth and have been seen up to a thousand meters (three thousand feet) deep, about the depth where water turns pitch black.

Though they look sleek and slippery, both species are covered in tooth-shaped scales called dermal denticles. These scales provide some protection and reduce drag and turbulence, helping them swim faster. In giant mantas the dermal denticles are longer and pointier, making them rougher to the touch than reef mantas, which are much smoother.

Mantas are famous for their alien-looking diamond-shaped body. Their eyes are located on the sides of their heads, giving them strong lateral vision. Their gills are located on their underbellies, and they have two horn-shaped cephalic fins, which they use to guide water and prey into their large mouths. Because of these fins, they are the only known vertebrates to have three paired appendages.

Unlike most other ray species, but similarly to the largest sharks, mantas are filter feeders and eat vast amounts of zooplankton. Because of this, their mouths are not located on the bottom of their heads, where they would be best located for catching prey from above, and instead are up front. As they swim, they open their massive mouths and funnel shrimp, copepods, decapod larvae, and other zooplankton into their stomachs. Often the packs will feed together, creating a large feeding train in areas rich with prey.

Being filter feeders, manta rays end up with a lot of the ocean in their mouths and their gill rakers, or filters, need to be cleaned regularly. Additionally, the filters in their gills are arranged in a way that minimizes filter-clogging and helps them catch hundreds of thousands of small prey.

Their filtration system allows for zooplankton to flow over the gills, rather than going through them. This causes their food to bounce off the filter and into their stomachs, while the water is flushed out.

The search for food is never-ending and mantas form massive groups of up to 1,500 members to look for their next meal. It's during these group trips that their most amazing behavior usually happens.

Like several ray species, mantas leap out of the water like a spaceship emerging from the ocean.

The reason for this fantastically delightful display of power remains a mystery. It's possible they launch themselves out of the

water as part of a mating ritual, to communicate with other rays, to get rid of parasites, or even just for fun. Whatever the reason, it's one of the most magical behaviors in nature.

Unfortunately, both the giant oceanic manta and the reef manta are threatened species. Recently, they have been caught in increasing numbers to satisfy the demand for their gill rakers in the traditional Chinese medical market.

A kilogram of gill rakers can sell for five hundred dollars.

Merchants market these gill rakers as a way to rid your body of toxins, but this isn't supported by science, and, possibly even more frustratingly, it isn't even supported by traditional Chinese medical texts.

Ocean conservationists claim that this new demand for gills rakers has been manufactured to make up for the lessened demand for shark fin.

Mantas have low reproductive rates, and their overfishing has decimated their populations by 80 percent in some areas.

Fortunately, some countries are working to protect them. Indonesia has banned the fishing of manta rays, as they discovered that a living manta ray is worth up to two thousand times more than a dead one.

A dead manta ray may sell for five hundred dollars, but a living manta ray can produce up to a million dollars throughout its lifespan in tourism, as thousands of divers go into their waters for a chance to see these gentle giants up close.

Both species of manta ray are found in Indonesia, and this massive conservation area will hopefully begin to see a boom in their numbers. And as they become protected in other areas, we hope to keep seeing them leap out of the surf for many years to come.

Chapter 2
Secretary Bird

Don't let this bird's delicate looks distract you. The secretary bird has some serious kick!

The secretary bird is one of the most beautiful and widespread birds in sub-Saharan Africa. They're found strutting around in open grasslands and savannas across the continent.

Just because they're drop-dead gorgeous doesn't mean they aren't stone-cold killers. Everything about their biology is designed for hunting dangerous prey–particularly venomous snakes.

They have legs for days but they're stomping machines that kick with deadly accuracy. When they find a snake, secretary birds go for the head and stomp with ferocious speed.

Their stomps can produce forces 195 Newton: that's equivalent to five times their body weight.

Their fashion-forward plumage serves as a distraction. When hunting they shake their tail feathers and wings to get the snake's attention away from their legs to prevent them from biting them.

Some reports even suggest that they're at least partially immune to snake venom!

As a secondary safety measure, their contact time with the snake is about fifteen milliseconds. That's ten times faster than the blink of an eye, and more importantly, faster than a snake's reaction time.

Blink and you miss it. Ten times!

Their beautiful eyes have luscious eyelashes. These are modified feathers that filter debris when they're stomping and kicking up dust.

Maybe it's an evolutionary trait that evolved over hundreds of thousands of years to protect their most important sensory organ, or maybe it's Maybelline.

In any case these killers have the prettiest peepers in the animal kingdom and have been turning heads for thousands of years.

Ancient Egyptians admired them and featured them in their art and building decorations. Bas-reliefs depicting secretary birds were most recently discovered at the temple of Hetupset. The amazing thing is that there are no secretary birds in Egypt, so Egyptian artists might have traveled to see them, or pharaohs imported them to grace the royal palaces. In any case, the artists were so awestruck by their beauty that they carved the beautiful birds in stone for posterity.

Thousands of years later, European naturalists were also struck by their elegance.

They were originally named Sagittarius, which is Greek for "Archer," because of their refined and deliberate gait. As well as for their head feathers, which resemble the arrows sticking out of an archer's quiver.

Nobody knows for sure how the name changed from Sagittarius to the less impressive secretary bird. The leading theories are that they reminded English naturalists of their secretaries, who used to use goose quill pens and put them in their heads when they were not writing.

The other theory is that it comes from the Arabic word sakr-et-air, which means "hunter bird." And that might be a more accurate name given their snake-killing abilities.

Despite their stork-like physique, their closest relatives are birds of prey, like eagles and hawks. And like birds of prey, they have a special ability: they can squirt their feces instead of dropping it. Wonderful.

Secretary birds are basically eagles on stilts and can be up to 1.3 meters (four feet) tall. Yet, these tall birds are surprisingly light—at just about four kilograms (nine pounds). Their hollow bones help them grow tall and statuesque without making them too heavy for flying.

They're not as graceful in the air as their eagle cousins, but they can fly at heights of up to 300 meters (10,000 feet). But when you look this fly on land, there's little reason to leave the ground.

With such extravagant beauty you would expect them to be avian Casanovas but they're more like Romeos and Juliets.

During courtship males perform elaborate flight displays to impress the females in the area. If a female likes a male, they'll form a monogamous couple and will build a large nest on an acacia tree. The nests are about 2.5 meters (nine feet) wide, spacious enough for the two secretary birds and a couple of babies.

To feed their babies, secretary birds carry their prey in their mouths rather than in their feet. Their legs are deadly stomping machines, and their talons are sharp enough to shred prey to pieces, but their foot muscles are not strong enough to carry heavy prey.

Unfortunately, even though secretary birds can lay up to four eggs, usually only two babies survive. The chicks have to compete with each other for the food their parents bring home. This conflict is also known as Cainism, after Cain and Abel.

Parental care doesn't end at the nest. After eighty days, the babies fledge and start leaving the nest, but the parents stick around until the young learn how to hunt by themselves. Once they're fully grown and pretty, they disperse and start their own beautiful families.

Chapter 3
Snapping Turtles

The face of a snapping turtle is the last thing a lot of fish see before they die. It's not pretty.

Snapping turtles is an umbrella term for five large predatory turtles across two genera: *Macrochelys* and *Chelydra*.

Chelydra contains the common snapping turtle, the Mexican snapping turtle, and the South American snapping turtle, while *Macrochelys* contains the alligator snapping turtle and the Suwannee Snapping Turtle.

These turtles are all large, and they're only found in the wild in the Americas.

While the two genera share similar characteristics, they aren't closely related and only share a name due to their similar behavior: the snapping.

To hunt, alligator snapping turtles have a vermiform—a tongue that resembles a worm to attract fish. The turtle sits at the bottom of the river or lake with its mouth open. It lies still—except for its tongue, which it wiggles around, mimicking fish prey. Then, it waits for a fish to follow the lure and swim into its mouth.

Their bite is fast and strong enough that if they don't swallow the fish whole, they're sure to decapitate them. Their diet is made up primarily of fish, but they also eat birds, small mammals, baby gators, and other turtles.

There is a lot of misinformation out there about the strength of an alligator snapping turtle's bite. Some cite them as having bites as strong as an alligator. They don't.

Their bite is much closer to the strength of a human—which is plenty, especially when combined with a sharp beak. It's enough power to bite off a finger.

Yet despite this vicious appearance and powerful jaws, they are chill, unlike common snapping turtles, which are the bullies of the pond.

This may be due to their different hunting strategies. Alligator snapping turtles are ambush hunters, while common snapping turtles are chase hunters. It could also be due to their size. A fully grown adult alligator snapping turtle has few predators, while the smaller common snapping turtle is more often on the defense. Being aggressive might be necessary to fend off predators.

Alligator snapping turtles are more intimidating in almost every regard; the common snapping turtle has a more fearsome tail. It has a series of bone plates that give it a saw-tooth appearance. It almost looks like a dragon's tail—more impressive than that of its beefy, smooth-tailed cousins.

Despite being chase hunters, common snapping turtles are terrible swimmers, preferring to walk along the bottom. They spend most of their lives in the water, only ever leaving when basking in the sun or laying eggs. In fact, they spend so much time in the water that they can often be seen with full heads of hair—the hair being algae.

Alligator snapping turtles are the larger of two, measuring up to sixty-five centimeters (twenty-five inches) long, and in extreme cases, weighing up to one hundred kilograms (220 pounds). Though those massive numbers come from turtles in captivity, and in the wild an average adult male will only weigh up to forty kilograms (ninety pounds).

Common snapping turtles, on the other hand, are smaller. They measure up to forty-five centimeters (seventeen inches) long, and in the wild weigh up to sixteen kilograms (thirty-five pounds).

Alligator snapping turtles are submarine tanks. Once they reach their full size, they become immune to most predators. Only large gators are powerful enough to crack their shells. They certainly do their namesake justice.

They also have claws the length of human fingers, highly ridged carapaces, and a sharp triceratops-like beak, which they use to tear into prey.

They command the ponds and streams they live in and spend most of their time in areas shallow enough that they can sit with only the tips of their noses sticking out of the water. Any prey that comes too close to them is in danger.

But this is only later in their lives. As hatchlings they're vulnerable and have high mortality rates. They break out of their ping-pong ball-like eggs toward the end of the summer, with the entire litter often hatching at the same time. Then it's a mad rush for these tiny turtles to get clear of the river banks and beaches and dive into the water without being eaten.

The water provides some shelter, but there are still large birds, reptiles, and fish that can catch them. Only the luckiest of the lucky survive to be big enough to ward off predators and humans.

Alligator snapping turtles are currently threatened due to overharvesting for meat, the exotic pet trade, and habitat degradation, though the situation for snapping turtles is better than it was fifty years ago.

For a long time, turtle soup was a mainstay at North American restaurants. It was praised for its complexity of flavors. But as turtle numbers plummeted and indoor plumbing reduced the need to go to creeks and ponds to grab fresh water and hunt turtles, it became unprofitable to look for turtles. At the same time,

factory farming of chickens, cows, and pigs created a steady supply of cheap meat, and turtles transitioned from being seen as a food species to being seen as cute and benevolent creatures.

If you see one on the road, make sure to help it cross. They were close to extinction and they're still recovering. It's the least we can do for a species that fed many of our ancestors.

Chapter 4
FROGFISHES

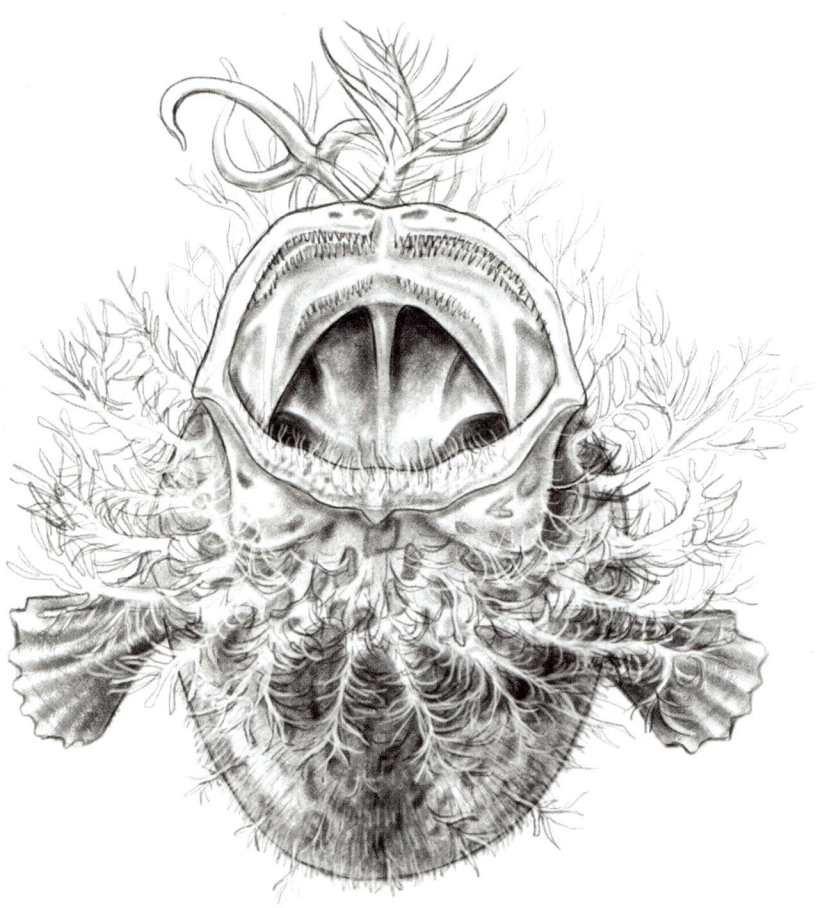

At the bottom of warm seas all over the world, the curious frogfish waddles along. It is a fish, but its slow movement, stubby pectoral fins, and huge head give it an almost amphibian appearance. It is one of the most appropriately named fish in the ocean.

There are around fifty frogfish species in the world, ranging in size from five to forty centimeters long (two to fifteen inches).

They live in waters where the temperature is about 20 degrees Celsius (70 degrees Fahrenheit) and thrive in and around corals at depths of twenty to a hundred meters (sixty-five to three hundred feet) deep.

Their bodies are not built for speed. They're poor swimmers and use their pectoral and pelvic fins to walk along the ocean floor. They're unusual looking whose entire biology is geared toward helping them blend in with their environments.

Frogfish are ambush predators. Their strategy consists of lying still on the ocean floor and waiting for prey to come close enough for them to strike. Their colour and texture resemble the corals and algae of their ecosystems, making them almost invisible to predators and prey alike.

If they move to a new environment, it will take them a couple of weeks to fully change to the right colour to match their surroundings. Their disguise is realistic enough that sea snails sometimes climb on them, mistaking them for inanimate objects.

Some look like coral and others resemble sea sponges, but possibly the most amazing of them all is the hairy frogfish, which have long strains of skin called spinules. These are meant to resemble algae-covered coral.

When these fishies have their camo on, it's time to go hunting. To attract prey they use a lure. Their first spine tilts forward and has been modified to look like a delicious worm, which they wiggle around for added realism. In some species, like the hairy frogfish, the "worm" also works as a chemical lure. That means that to fish, it not only looks like a worm but also smells like a worm.

Naive fish and crustaceans will get enticed by the promise of an easy meal, and when they get close enough, the frogfish pulls the trigger.

Though they're slow in pretty much every aspect of their lives, frogfish have the fastest bite of all vertebrates. They can open their mouth, suck in a fish, close their mouths, and swallow in just a few milliseconds—several times faster than the blink of an eye.

If you're a prey item, you go from thinking you're about to get a meal to being in the stomach of a frogfish faster than you can even think, "That's no moon."

When a frogfish opens its mouth, its mouth grows twelve times its original size. This is such a quick movement that the fish creates a vacuum in its mouth, forcing water to rush into the mouth and pulling the prey in.

Since their mouths are so large, they can eat prey almost as big as them. To accommodate such large meals, they can inflate themselves like a pufferfish. It's their version of undoing the button of your pants on Thanksgiving.

Frogfish can also do this stretching ability when threatened by a predator. They will absorb water to make themselves look larger and more dangerous than they are.

If this fails, they have another ace up their sleeve: jet propulsion.

The water that they absorb to make themselves bigger can be expelled through holes behind their pectoral gills. It's basically like inflating a balloon and then releasing it without tying a knot. It's not elegant, but it works.

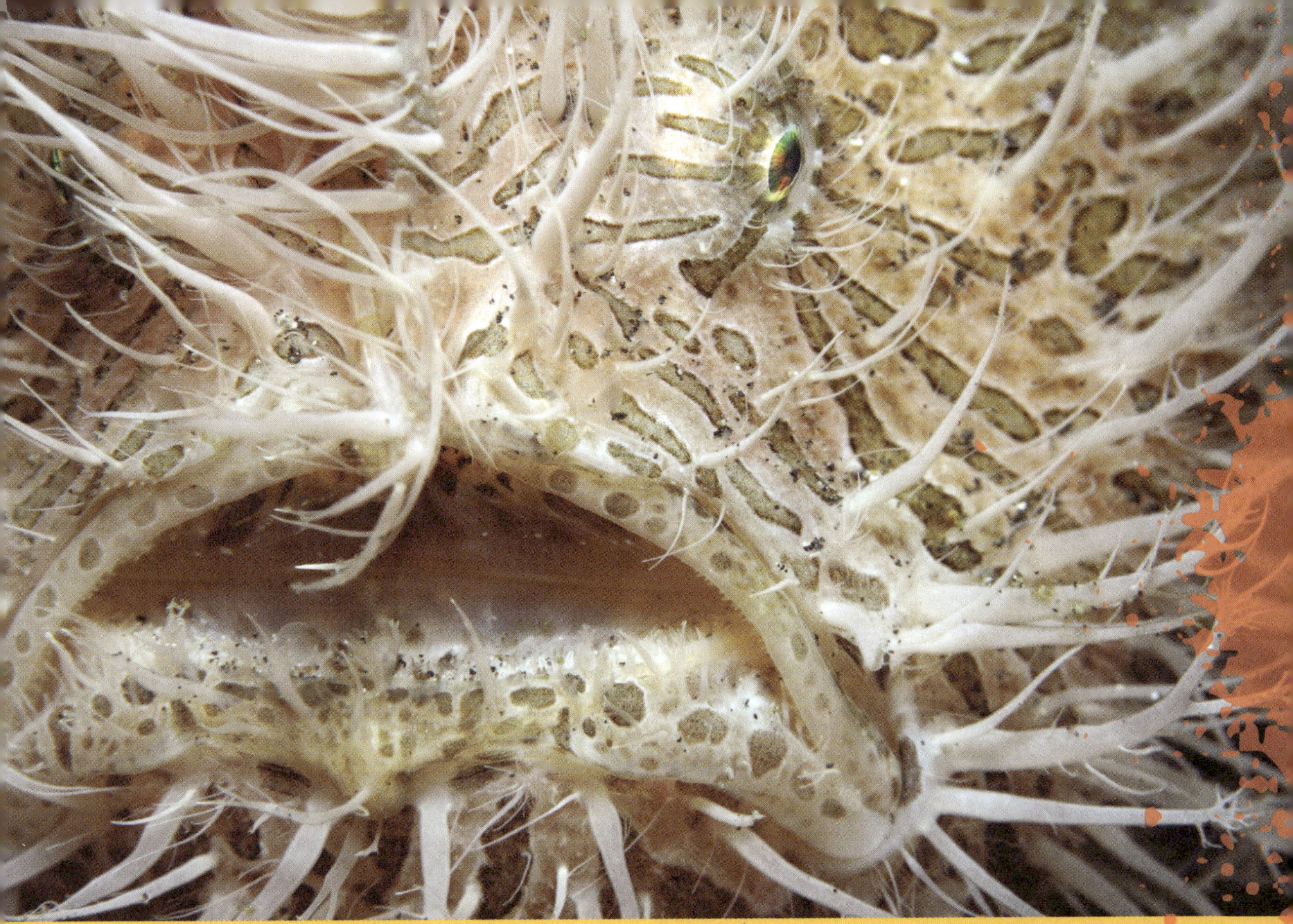

This method of locomotion is also used when mating.

Being ambush predators, frogfish don't spend much time socializing. They don't generally tolerate other frogfish except when it's time to fertilize eggs. Females are often larger than males, so a male can't do anything but follow a female around at a safe distance until she's ready to lay her eggs.

This process can take up to two days and culminates with the female jetting upwards toward the surface and releasing the eggs at the highest point. The eggs come out in egg rafts, which makes it easier for the male to fertilize. Up to 180,000 eggs can come out at the same time.

Unfortunately, like many fish, several species of frogfish are struggling. Species that live in coral reefs are at risk due to coral bleaching, which happens when water gets too hot for the coral to host algae. This starts a domino effect that leads to crashes in biodiversity.

If you still want to see frogfish in the wild, one of the best places is in the warm waters of the Indian Ocean. Go check them out while they're still abundant!

Chapter 5
Basking Shark

This is one of the great white shark's closest relatives. It is larger, heavier, and has a bigger jaw than its famous cousin. But instead of traveling the world terrorizing seals, it prefers the simple life. It swims with its mouth open, eating plankton and catching some rays: sun rays.

This is the basking shark.

Basking sharks are real-life Leviathans—they're the second-largest sharks in the world.

Older adults can be over ten meters (thirty feet) long. The largest basking shark ever caught was twelve meters (forty feet) long and completely shattered the scale at a whopping sixteen tonnes.

That's about three African elephants combined!

Unfortunately, few specimens get that big anymore due to overfishing by the shark fin industry.

From afar, basking sharks look a lot like a great white. But this is how you can tell them apart.

Basking sharks have a long conical snout. Their scientific name, *Cetorhinus maximus*, means "the greatest marine monster with a big nose." Their mouths are huge and open wider than a great white's, but their teeth are smaller at just a few millimeters long.

The basking shark is also the only shark that has gigantic gills that almost encircle their head.

This combination of giant mouth and huge gills is an adaptation for life as a filter feeder.

The feeding strategy of these sharks consists of swimming slowly, at about three kilometers (two miles) an hour and eating microscopic plankton in the water column.

Despite their size they never attempt to hunt larger prey. Their teeth have become too small for them to be effective predators.

They catch some of their prey near the surface, and since they're so slow they look like they're just chilling in the sun with their mouths open. This is why they're called basking sharks.

Perhaps unsurprisingly due to their lifestyle, they have the smallest brains relative to body size among all sharks.

They don't have that much to do or think about in their daily life, just swim forward with their mouths open and let food fall into their bellies.

Basking sharks are ram feeders, which means that they can't suck in water and have to swim to push water through their gills. An average basking shark can filter five hundred tonnes of water every hour.

To catch plankton they have gill rakers that lead the solid plankton into the stomach. As the solid matter approaches the gills, the gill rakers create a bit of turbulence so that plankton slides over the gills without getting stuck. Then, the water is forced out of the gills.

About 75 percent of their diet consists of zooplankton, and they have to travel vast distances to find it.

Basking sharks have been tagged and tracked and they've been found to travel thousands of kilometers every season at an incredibly slow speed.

It's the most boring cruise in the world, but there is a fun part to their travels.

These travels are the only times basking sharks get to meet other basking sharks, sometimes up to a hundred of them at a time. They get pretty riled up for a filter feeder.

When males are around females they perform unusual behaviors such as breaching, jumping out of the water, and nibbling females for attention.

Unfortunately, mating has not been observed yet. But someday soon we'll be able to witness this elusive event that has puzzled scientists for decades.

Basking sharks only have about five pups every two or three years. This low reproductive rate, combined with overfishing, puts them at risk of extinction. They're targeted for their meat, fins for soup, and liver oil for cosmetics, but they're also caught as bycatch. They're currently considered a threatened species and their trade is regulated through the CITES program.

In 2019, Canada became the first country to ban the importation of shark fins. Hopefully as more countries follow suit we'll see all shark species' numbers rebound.

Chapter 6
Chimaeras

In Greek mythology, the chimaera was a fire-breathing hybrid of a lion, a goat, and a snake. This fantastical mythical creature has inspired the name of one of the spookiest species of the depths of the ocean.

Chimaeras, also known as ghost sharks, are the forgotten members of the cartilaginous fish class, Chondrichthyes. When people talk about these fish, they usually only talk about sharks, rays, and skates, and forget about these deep sea Frankensteins.

The majority of chimaera live in the depths of oceans around the world–thriving in depths of 200 to 2,600 meters (600 to 8,500 feet), though a few species, like the fantastically named *Chimaera monstrosa*, live in shallower waters, around 50 meters (150 feet) deep.

The chimaera's closest living relatives are sharks, but they parted ways 400 million years ago—about 10 million years before our ancestors emerged from the water.

They haven't changed all that much since then. Chimaeras are the most primitive cartilaginous fish.

While they still bear some resemblance to sharks, they can be easily told apart. One of their most prominent differences is their gills—sharks can have up to seven gill slits, while chimaera only have one. Their single gill slit is covered by a hard flap called an operculum.

Like their shark cousins, chimaera don't have any bones in their body, and their skeleton is made of cartilage. This makes studying their history difficult because cartilage doesn't fossilize how bone does.

We know these are not defenseless ghosts. Chimaera come equipped with a venomous dorsal spine to defend themselves most. This weapon is located on their backs, and it's made of modified scale tissue that breaks off after use. Thankfully for chimaera, they can quickly grow a replacement.

This dorsal spine is effective and produces incredibly painful stings in humans and other vertebrates. Chimaera venom is powerful enough to cause necrosis, hallucinations, and temporary paralysis. You do not want to mess with these ghosts, especially underwater.

There are three chimaera families to keep in mind next time you're in deep water.

The first contains the plough-nosed chimaera, or elephant fish. They get their name from a fleshy appendage sticking out of their face.

This nose-plough measures up to 125 centimeters (50 inches) long and is used to find bottom-dwelling prey, like sea urchins, mollusks, and crabs. This tool is lined with electroreceptors, which help locate hidden prey by sensing electric fields created by muscle movements. Even if their prey sits perfectly still, their hearts give them away.

Then, the chimaera strikes, crushing their prey with their broad, flat teeth.

While elephant fish may have the most specialized electroreceptors, all species of chimaera have sensory organs used to detect electric fields to find prey. You can see them by looking closely at the chimaera's face, which is dotted with electro-sensory organs.

The second family is the short-nosed chimaera, or ratfish. Their snout is shorter than their plough-nosed cousins, and they have a longer and skinnier tail—hence their name.

Finally, the long-nosed chimaeras. These fish have long, paddle-shaped noses and resemble ghosts. They are also known as spookfish, for obvious reasons.

Hopefully as they become more well-known they'll become Halloween staples and marine biologists' favorite weirdos.

Chapter 7
Weaver Ants

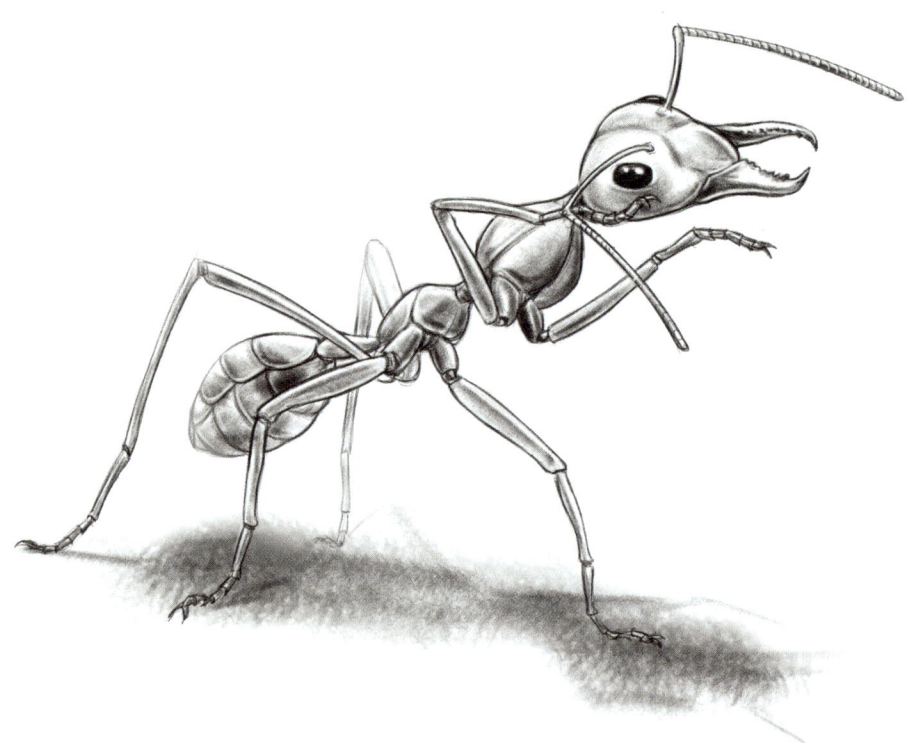

Ants are the architects of the animal world. Millions of years before we built the first cities, ants were already building gigantic megastructures.

Most ant species build elaborate networks of tunnels and chambers, but weaver ants have colonized the tree canopy and built amazing cities out of leaves.

There are two species of weaver ants in the world: *Oecophylla longinoda*, found in Eastern Africa, and *Oecophylla smaragdina*, found in Asia and Oceania.

They live at the top of the tree canopy, safe from predators. Their colonies are huge, often containing over half a million ants, and they build their nests with tree leaves. These extend over hundreds of square meters and can occupy several trees.

And all of this is built by tiny worker ants eight millimeters (0.3 inches) long. They're about the size of a grain of rice.

When looking for new areas to expand the colony, worker ants test leaves by bending them and aligning them with other nearby leaves. If the leaves have the right flexibility and location, other workers join in to help attach the leaves together. They grab one leaf with their front legs, another with their hind legs, and pull the leaves together.

WEAVER ANTS 39

Often leaves are too far apart for one line of ants to hold together, so weaver ants solve this problem by grabbing each other by the waist, creating ant chains.

They're the world's only useful conga lines.

When two leaves are touching it's time to sew them together. To do this they use an unconventional source of silk: their own babies.

Larvae from many ant species produce silk to make cocoons for themselves, but weaver ant larvae forgo the protection of a cocoon for the security of a safe shelter. That's because the colony's worker ants carry them to the construction site and use them as glue guns.

The larvae are held in the worker's mandibles and are softly squeezed while the worker moves back and forth from one leaf to another. They'll continue with several leaves until a ball of leaves, ranging in size from a tennis ball to a volleyball, is created.

In return for their services, the larvae are fed and taken care of until they're old and mature enough to become construction workers.

Building a nest is just the start. Maintaining these leaf-ball cities in the canopy requires lots of work and constant vigilance. Weaver ants constantly expand their colony; in case one ball gets knocked down, there's always a backup.

The queen lives at the center of the colony, while elderly workers live in the periphery, catching any prey that wanders in, and protecting it from invaders. It's said that while humans send their young men to war, weaver ants send their old ladies.

But not every foreigner is unwelcome in a weaver ant colony. Small insects such as mealybugs and scale insects are protected as they secrete a delicious and nutritious substance called honeydew. These insects are sometimes taken to designated pens where they're fed and milked. They're like the cows of the ants. This is an example of ranching in the animal kingdom.

When they're not looking after their livestock, weaver ants are usually preparing for chemical warfare. Formic acid is their weapon of choice

when fighting invaders or killing prey. Their bites are famously painful and they're even capable of killing much larger animals, like lizards and birds.

They're so good at defending their territory that some people in Southeast Asia use them as a defense mechanism for their crops. Weaver ant nests are placed in trees around crops and, in some cases, in the crops themselves to attack parasites and other insects that could harm the plants.

This ant-keeping knowledge has been passed on to thousands of hobbyists around the world who have started weaver ant colonies at home. Colonies can be started with just a couple of queens. They will lay eggs that turn into workers. The workers expand the colony little by little and, as it gets bigger, it becomes more efficient and able to support more larvae.

If you open a nest you'll see smaller workers who take care of the larvae. These are about half the size of the big workers. They're the nannies of the colony.

In other ant species there are a lot of tiny workers and a few big soldiers. Weavers are the opposite. There's a lot more big workers than small ones. This is because weaver ants do a lot more specialized construction work than other ants and the biggest ants are needed to do the heavy lifting.

These legendary ants are so common in Southeast Asia that they're not only used for crop protection but also as a source of food. They're full of protein and their formic acid gives them a tangy flavor.

Anyone interested in weaver ant tapenade?

Chapter 8
Millipedes

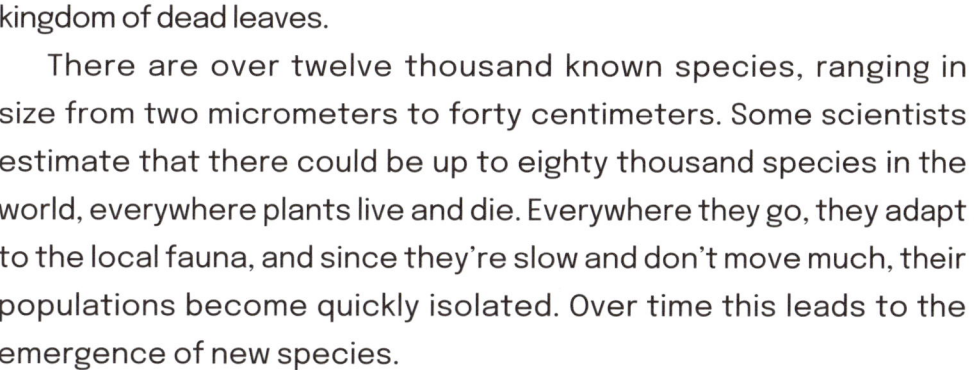

Millipedes are some of the most successful invertebrates on Earth. If you're outdoors you're likely a stone's throw away from one. Turn over any large dead piece of bark in the forest and you're likely to find one. Despite being generally easy prey, they thrive all over the world and have built a kingdom of dead leaves.

There are over twelve thousand known species, ranging in size from two micrometers to forty centimeters. Some scientists estimate that there could be up to eighty thousand species in the world, everywhere plants live and die. Everywhere they go, they adapt to the local fauna, and since they're slow and don't move much, their populations become quickly isolated. Over time this leads to the emergence of new species.

Their name means "thousand-legged," but unfortunately there are no known millipedes with that many legs. The record-holder for the most legs is *Illacme plenipes*, which can have up to 750 legs! They were considered extinct until 2012, when they were rediscovered in California. The most amazing thing about these millipedes is that they pack all their legs in a three-centimeter-long body.

The silver medalist is another California millipede, *Illacme tobine*. They *only* have 414 legs, but they make up for it by having two hundred poison glands and four penises.

The largest millipede in the world, the giant African millipede can be up to forty centimeters long and has 256 legs.

On the other side of the spectrum are pill millipedes, also known as roly polies, pill bugs, potato bugs, and slaters, among many other names. These little guys only have about seventy legs, and compared to their cousins they save a lot of money on shoes.

Some people consider millipedes a nuisance when they see them in our gardens, but it might have been we who took over their land. Millipedes are some of the oldest land animals on the planet. They're over 400 million years old. The oldest penis on record was found in a millipede fossil, and the largest land-dwelling invertebrates ever were the millipedes of the carboniferous.

During that era, there was a lot more carbon in the air, which led to giant insects and arachnids, but none as large as the *Arthopleura* millipedes, which grew to over two meters in length. You could ride it like a pony!

Modern millipedes are much smaller and are commonly mistaken for their more aggressive cousins, the centipedes, but there are some important differences between the two. The main one is that centipedes are venomous and carnivorous, while most millipedes eat dead plant matter exclusively and only some are poisonous.

The easiest way to tell them apart is by looking at their legs. Millipede legs are at the bottom of their bodies, while centipede legs are attached to the sides of their body. Millipedes have four legs on each segment while centipedes only have two. And despite the leg count advantage,

millipedes are slower than centipedes and are better built for burrowing than running.

Millipede legs might not be the fastest out there, but they have a more crucial job than running. They moonlight as reproductive organs. Some of their legs become penises as they grow and moult. The location of the sexual organs depends on the species, but most species have them in the seventh segment.

During copulation the male and female touch undersides while the male deposits a sperm capsule in the female's genital openings, which are usually in the third segment. The female then lays up to three hundred eggs, which soon hatch and start munching on leaf debris.

Their slow and quiet life gets interrupted frequently by predators. Animals from every order eat millipedes. They're an easy catch despite many species having powerful chemical defenses. Some assassin bugs are millipede specialists and are immune to their poison. Mammals can feel the effects of the poison, but some, like coatis and meerkats, are aware of their toxicity and rub the millipedes on the floor to wipe off the poison before eating them.

Red-fronted lemurs have come up with a better use for the poison: medicine. Instead of wasting the poison, they rub them on their genitals and anuses. This is believed to be a form of self-medication, as the poison helps them get rid of genital parasites and prevent itching. They also eat them to kill intestinal parasites.

Other lemurs have found a more recreational way of using millipedes. Black lemurs catch red millipedes and get them to release their poison. Then they rub them on their body to kill parasites, but also lick them and suck on them. This makes the lemur salivate copiously and then get high.

You've probably seen hundreds of millipedes, but if you want to see the most unique one you have to head to the sequoia forests of California. There you'll find psychedelic-looking, cyanide-producing *Mytoxia* millipedes. The chemicals in their bodies produce light, and at night you can see constellations of them illuminating the forest floor.

One more thing for the bucket list!

Chapter 9

Diving Beetles

Diving beetles are some of the most specialized insects in the world. At different points in their life cycle they're voracious tadpole hunters, holders of the most unusual eyes in the animal kingdom, and flying scuba divers.

Diving beetles are found all over the world in bodies of water with leafy cover. They have colonized most ponds and streams in warm and temperate climates. There are over four thousand species and they range in size from about one to five centimeters long.

You might see them at your nearest brook. Most of them are brown or black but some of the more stylish species rock the polka dot look. You can tell them apart by their large and hairy legs that they use to swim and catch prey.

Diving beetles are masters of the land, water, and air. They spend most of their lives underwater, though they're good fliers and will go from pond to pond looking for new sources of food. This ability to fly is especially important to species in warmer climates as their ponds dry up in the summer.

To avoid predators such as birds and dragonflies, they fly at night and rely on chemoreception to find new ponds. Once they find a new pond they dive down and look for vegetation. Their long and powerful hind legs propel them as they look for the perfect piece of vegetation of rock to cling to. If live prey or a carcass drift nearby, they'll pounce on it and devour it.

When it comes to diving beetles, most things are on the menu, as they're often rushing to get enough energy to moult, pupate, or reproduce. Mosquito larvae, tadpoles, and carrion of larger vertebrates are their most common prey and they'll often gang up to eat their prey. Even large crickets are readily eaten if they happen to fall into the water.

The most amazing diving beetle is possibly the sunburst diving beetle. They were just discovered in 1996 and, since then, they have become one of the most popular insects in zoos and aquaria.

Their beautiful colouration is a warning to predators. In the back of their head they have glands that secrete a noxious milky substance. Most predators avoid these little guys, but their defenses are especially effective against pond fish as their defense chemicals contain fish-deterrent steroids.

The males also have tiny suction cups in their frontal limbs to help them attach themselves to rocks and to stick themselves to females for more convenient access during mating.

Their name, of course, comes from their self-contained underwater breathing apparatus. They're literal scuba divers. They can get air from the surface and make a bubble under their wings. The bubble is also known as a physical gill and extends toward the back of the animal, where its breathing holes are located.

The amazing thing about the bubble is that, unlike scuba tanks, it can take oxygen from the surrounding water. This gives them extra diving time, but there isn't enough oxygen in the water to keep the bubble oxygenated indefinitely, so eventually it runs out of oxygen. The beetle then releases its bubble and goes to the surface to get a new one.

Unfortunately for the beetle, their bubble is also home to parasites. Mites attach themselves to their underwings and rely on the beetle's air to survive. If the beetle dies in the water, the mites die too as they can't live anywhere else.

Their association goes back over one hundred million years and it's one of the oldest extant examples of obligate parasitism, where a parasite can only survive on the resources of a particular host.

Diving beetles are one of the rare examples in nature where babies are more active and interesting than grownups. Their larvae are called water tigers due to their unmitigated ferociousness.

Water tigers are longer than adult diving beetles and have huge pincers to catch prey. Their hunting strategy consists mostly of waiting for tadpoles, glassworms, and other pond critters to swim too close. Then the water tiger attacks and chases the prey with quick undulating motions.

Tadpoles seem to be their favorite prey. Adult diving beetles often lay their eggs on frog eggs so that when the water tigers emerge, they have a ready source of food.

After they gorge themselves with delicious baby frogs and are ready to pupate, they come out of the water. They bury themselves in mud to undergo their complete metamorphosis.

The water tigers of the diving sunburst beetle have some of the most unusual eyes in the animal kingdom. They are the only known example of truly bifocal vision. Their eyes have bifocal lenses connected to two separate retinas. The lenses can create two separate sharp images, each of which goes to a different retina.

Unfortunately, the precise function of this arrangement is unknown, but it might help them to keep an eye on distant predators, and the same eye on nearby prey. It's a busy life being a water tiger.

Chapter 10
GHARIAL

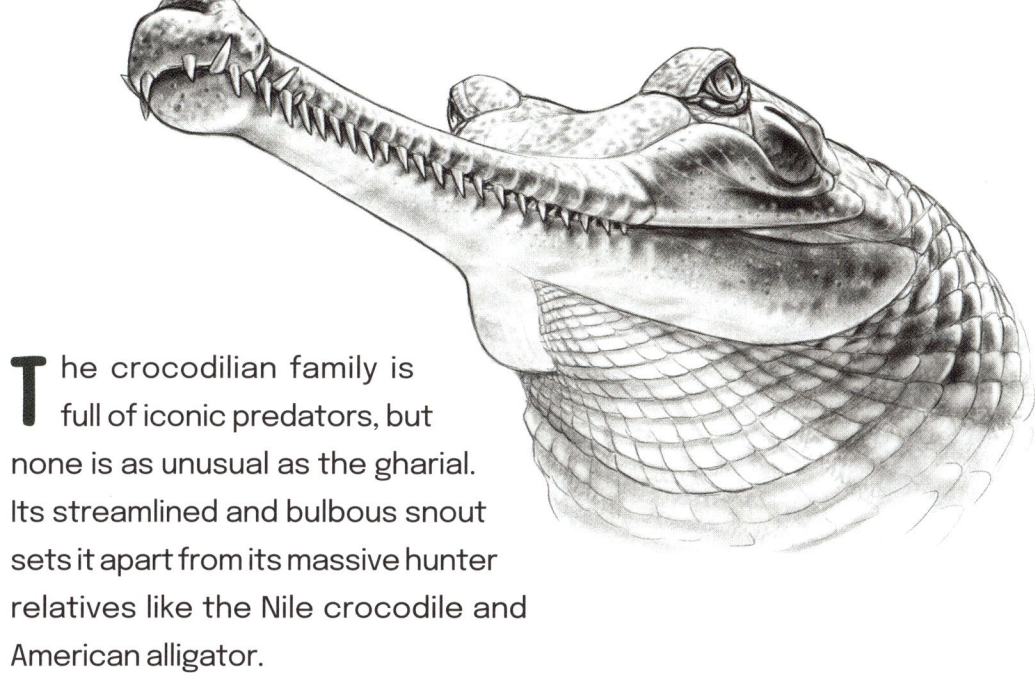

The crocodilian family is full of iconic predators, but none is as unusual as the gharial. Its streamlined and bulbous snout sets it apart from its massive hunter relatives like the Nile crocodile and American alligator.

Like their ancient cousins, gharials have been on Earth for over a hundred million years. They once shared the planet with the dinosaurs of the Cretaceous. Today they're found in India and Nepal, where they share their territory with the deadly mugger crocodiles.

Their defining feature is their long, thin snouts with a little bulb at the end. This, as you might expect, is an adaptation to kill.

Gharials are fish specialists and need to have an exceedingly quick bite to catch their agile aquatic prey. Their thin snout cuts through the water with little resistance. Wide-snouted crocs have stronger bites but aren't nearly as fast as gharials. It's like the difference between rowing with oars and rowing with a sword.

Other crocodilians, such as the Malayan false gharial, which lacks a bulb at the end of the snout, are pescatarians but none are as large and fast as the gharial.

Gharials have relatively weak bites, but that doesn't mean they're not lethal. They have over a hundred needle-like teeth that interlock like a zipper, stabbing and trapping fish in the gharial's mouth.

Gharials usually ambush their prey, waiting for an unsuspecting fish to swim too close to their deadly snouts, but they have also been observed rapidly shaking in pursuit of prey. They also eat other aquatic prey such as crustaceans and frogs, especially when young. There are reports of gharials catching small dogs and goats, but fish make up most of their diet.

This doesn't mean that you should approach them. Gharials are huge. They're larger than Nile and American crocodiles. Males are about 4.5 meters long on average, with some size kings getting to over six meters in length.

If you do see one, thankfully there's a good chance that it will quickly run away from you. In fact, they don't like to encounter any large land animals at all.

They're the most aquatic of all large crocodilians and spend most of their life in the water. They only come out to raise their core temperature and prefer small river islands over the river banks.

It's not hard to see why they prefer water over land. Their arms are relatively weak and can't lift their own weight and, unlike other crocodilians, they can't sprint on land.

But underwater they're as agile as a dolphin. Their webbed feet and long flattened tails give them great swimming power. Their nose sticks out just enough for them to breathe while they're almost fully submerged, but this isn't the bulbous tip's only use.

The bulb resembles an Indian clay pot called a ghara, which gives gharials their name. It lacks bones or cartilage, but it has echo chambers that act as a resonator.

Only males have this bulb, which makes gharials the only sexually dimorphic crocodilian. They start growing them before they're sexually mature, when they're about ten years old.

They can make a popping noise to communicate with other gharials as far as five hundred meters away. Their sound is unique to each gharial, which makes it easier for them to know who's saying what. Males also use it to make a far-reaching buzzing noise to call females, and, during courtship, they blow bubbles, which females find adorable.

After mating, the female travels up to two hundred kilometers upstream to find breeding sites and makes a nest near the river bank and lays her eggs. Gharials make the largest eggs among crocodilians, about the size of a baseball. They usually lay around forty eggs per clutch, but large healthy females can lay a lot more than that. The biggest clutch ever recorded had ninety-seven eggs.

Imagine carrying ninety-seven baseballs inside you. No thank you!

When the babies hatch, they call their mom, who digs out their nest and points them toward the water. Other crocodilians carry their babies to safety in their mouths, but gharial snouts are too chainsaw-like to do it safely.

Then the mom and a male will take care of the babies until the monsoon season. The male is not necessarily their father, and younger males often protect other males' babies. This might be kind of a parenthood internship until they're large enough to establish themselves as dominant breeding males.

In the meantime, they often carry them on their backs to protect them. Scientists believe that this is one of the cutest things on Earth, and I couldn't agree more. Babies are small, about the size of a squirrel!

Despite their large egg clutches and great parenting, gharials are critically endangered. Populations have crashed in the past hundred years and are less than 5 percent of what they used to be at the beginning of the twentieth century.

At their lowest numbers in the 1970s, studies showed that there were just over two hundred breeding adults in the whole world. Since then there have been conservation efforts that involve breeding gharials in captivity and releasing babies in the wild.

Unfortunately, numbers haven't improved as expected and there are still under a thousand adults in the wild. Habitat destruction due to mining and dam construction, gill-net fishing, and water contamination are the main reasons most reintroduced gharials never reach maturity.

Efforts to restore gharial populations are still ongoing, and hopefully with improved environmental conditions these speedy swimming chainsaws will be restored to their former glory.

Chapter 11
Coconut Crab

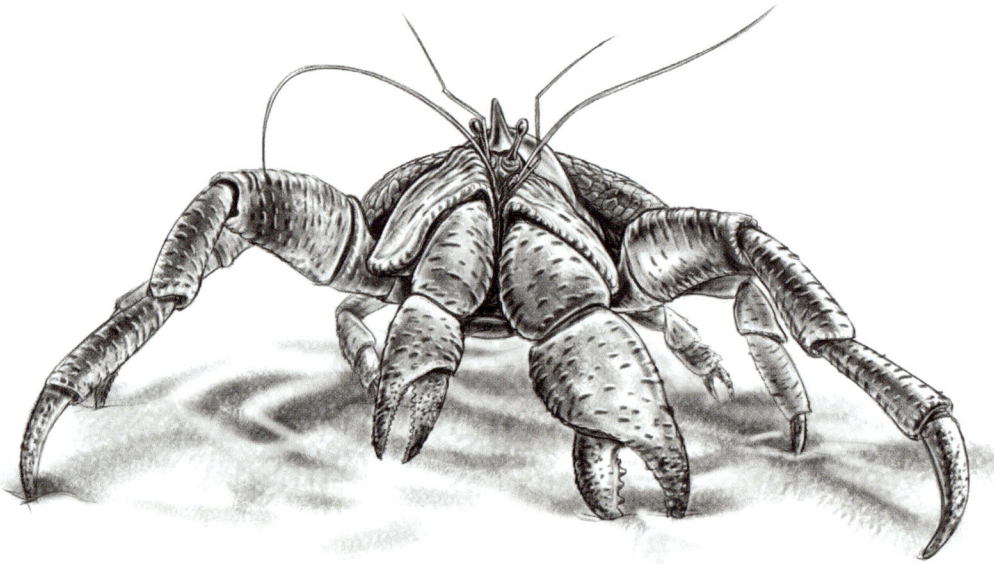

The coconut crab is the largest land invertebrate in the world. They get a bad reputation because they're humongous, have huge claws, and have been seen eating birds and kittens. But if you get past all of that, they're amazing creatures.

Let's start with the obvious. Coconut crabs are massive. They can have a leg span of over a meter and weigh over four kilograms. This might be the current physiological size limit for arthropods.

Back in the day there used to be larger land arthropods, including the fearsome eurypterid, which was two and half meters long. But as oxygen levels in the air dropped, their large bodies became unsustainable, as they're not as efficient at absorbing oxygen as vertebrates.

Coconut crabs are the biggest invertebrates we have, but if you want to see them you might have to travel far.

They're found on islands in the South Pacific and the Indian Ocean, with large populations living on Christmas Island and the Cook Islands. Their distribution aligns nicely with the distribution of the coconut palm. These crabs are surprisingly great climbers and often climb palm trees to grab coconuts, but, when possible, they prefer to eat nuts and fleshy fruits.

Some of those fruits, including the sea mango, have toxins that get stored in the crabs' bodies and make them poisonous to humans.

Their asymmetrical claws are among the largest in the animal kingdom, and for a yet unknown reason the left one is always larger than the right.

Coconut crabs have the strongest claw grip in the animal kingdom at 1,500 Newtons.

They're used for self-defense, hunting, and opening coconuts. To do this, they pull away the outer fibers in a process that might take days. Then they pierce holes through the eyes of the coconut with their thin and pointy legs, which makes it easier to break to access the meat.

Coconuts are so important to them, that in areas without coconuts they are about half the size of coconut crabs from areas with coconuts.

Though mostly vegetarian, coconut crabs will eat anything they can get their claws on. Carrion, rats, birds, and even smaller coconut crabs are consumed when available.

In one gruesome case, a coconut crab was observed eating a red-footed booby, a graceful seabird commonly found on the islands of the Pacific. The crab climbed a tree in the middle of the night. It approached a sleeping red-footed booby and grabbed it by the wing, breaking its bones. This caused the bird to fall to the ground.

The crab climbed down from the tree and grabbed the other wing, also breaking it. Then it started eating alive. The smell of blood attracted twenty other coconut crabs, which proceeded to have booby for dinner.

There's a morbid theory that the reason Amelia Earhart was never found was because coconut crabs dragged her to their burrows and ate her. This is most likely incorrect as we have no evidence of it, but it is right about the coconut crab's capacity to eat much larger animals.

Their sense of smell on land is advanced compared to other crustaceans, and they have convergently evolved an olfactory system similar to insects, with antennae full of chemoreceptors. These antennae help them find food and potential Valentine's Day dates, which for them is between May and September.

Males deposit a spermatophore on the abdomen of the female, which she uses to fertilize her eggs. When they're ready to hatch,

she goes to the water and releases them when the tide is high. The babies live as plankton for about a month, fully dependent on ocean currents for movement.

When they're a little older, they go to the bottom and use abandoned sea snail shells for protection. Then, within the first year of their life they go to land and lose their ability to breathe underwater.

If you find a coconut crab, do not throw it into the water! Just give it a good claw shake and send it on its way. We're kidding; do not touch their claws!

They then will continue growing for decades. We're still not sure at what age they reach their maximum size, but it's believed to be at least forty years of age, with some scientists claiming that they could grow until they're about 120 years old.

As they grow, like all crustaceans, coconuts crabs moult. They shed their exoskeleton and grow a new larger one. The new exoskeleton is initially soft, which makes them vulnerable for a few weeks after moulting.

This happens every year, and, to avoid harm, they dig a burrow to shed their old exoskeleton. Then they eat it to recoup nutrients and wait for the new one to harden.

I guess they really hate birthdays.

Unfortunately it's getting increasingly harder to find huge coconut crabs. They got this big because they had no natural predators on their islands. But humans and the animals they bring, such as dogs and pigs, have caused a rapid decline in their populations. They're now extinct in parts of their historical range, such as Madagascar and mainland Australia.

Hopefully, as we learn more about them, we can protect them better. But until then, we environmental protections and attitude changes toward them will help us boost their populations.

Chapter 12
CONDORS

Condors are some of the largest flying birds in the world. They evolved at a time when megafauna was common in the Americas and there was an abundant amount of carrion. They fed on mastodons, mammoths, and giant sloths. But as the great American giants died out due to climate change and human predation, most condors ran out of food.

Today only two condor species survive: the California condor and the Andean condor.

They're part of the New World Vulture family, and like their cousins, they soar for hundreds of kilometers every day in search of carrion.

The North American species used to be found from coast to coast. Unfortunately today they're only found in Arizona and California, where they feed mostly the carrion of deer, sheep, and large marine mammals that wash upon the shore of the Pacific coast.

The Andean condor, found in South America, feeds on dead llamas, guanacos, cetaceans, and other decaying livestock.

Both species are huge, but the South American species is slightly beefier. California condors have a wingspan of up to three meters and weigh up to ten kilograms, while Andean condors have a wingspan of 3.3 meters and can weigh up to fifteen kilograms.

This puts them among the largest flying birds in the world. Only great albatrosses and some pelican species have a larger wingspan, and only male kori bustards are heavier than the largest condors.

The condor's enormous wings help them glide without making much of an effort. They have been observed soaring for over an hour without flapping their wings. But compared to some of their extinct relatives, condors are little runts.

The most amazing of them was the giant terator, which might have had twice the wingspan and four times the weight of an Andean condor.

Condors being this huge means they have no predators when fully grown, but it also means they need a lot of food to survive. When looking for carrion, they look for smaller scavengers, such as turkey vultures and crows, to help them find food. Turkey vultures are particularly useful because they have one of the most developed chemoreception systems among birds, so they can sniff out carrion in forested areas.

Condors can go several days without eating, but when they find food they can eat several kilograms in one sitting. The condor's large beak can tear through thick skin more efficiently than a turkey vulture's. Once the condor has had its fill the turkey vulture and other scavengers can access food that they otherwise couldn't, so it's mutually beneficial.

The king looks after his people.

Part of the condor's regal fashion sense is the frill of feathers at the base of their neck. California condors have a black frill and on Andean condors, it is white. The South American condor also has a crown on their bald head.

Their featherless head is an adaptation for life as a scavenger. Having no hair or feathers makes it much easier to clean. It also exposes pathogens to dehydration and ultraviolet light at high altitudes. It's basically the same reason why kitchens aren't carpeted.

Their least majestic habit is the way they cool themselves off. They empty their cloacas on their feet. Uric acid found in their waste dries up on their legs, protects them from sunburns, and prevents skin dryness.

Though scary-looking and slightly macabre, these beautiful scavengers are great parents. When they're about six years old they become sexually mature and start looking for a partner. They mate for life and a couple can stay together for over fifty years.

They usually lay one or two eggs. Chicks hatch after two months of incubation. At six months of age they can fly on their own but stay with their parents until they're about two years old. By then, the parents are ready to lay new eggs, so the older siblings get kicked out.

Despite their careful parenting, California condors are critically endangered. In the '80s, the condor population of North America was in the double digits. A plan called the California Condor Recovery Plan was started and it consisted of catching all the wild condors and creating a breeding process in captivity.

Of course there were ethical, economic, and ecological concerns, but the plan went ahead and by 1987, all twenty-two living California condors were in captivity.

They were bred and the chicks were reared using puppets to prevent them from imprinting on humans.

A few years later, the first human-raised condors were reintroduced to the wild. Since then the populations have been growing steadily, but they still face challenges such as electric power lines, egg collection, lead poisoning from eating animals killed with lead bullets, and accidentally eating plastic.

Today there are more than 450 California condors, and their population grows every year.

The Andean condor is doing better. They're protected across their range as they are the national bird of seven South American countries. There are about ten thousand Andean condors, and about two-thirds of them are sexually mature.

Great job and thank you to all you who helped California condors back from the brink of death! And here's to more future successes!

Chapter 13
Pallas's Cat

Pallas's cats may look like cute and lazy house cats, but don't let that fool you. They have adapted to life in some of the most inhospitable places in the world. They're savvy hunters and amazing parents, a combination of skills that has helped them conquer a vast chunk of Asia, from the Mongolian deserts to the Himalayas.

But their charm goes beyond their survival skills. The Pallas's cat–or manul, as it's known in some places–has a unique feature that separates it from other small cats: weirdly human eyes.

If you look closely, you'll notice that Pallas's cats have round pupils instead of vertical slits, unlike other small cats. This gives them somewhat of a more expressive human look and is the reason why people on the internet have fallen in love with them.

Their round eyes and furrowed brows make them look like they don't like Mondays. If anything these guys are the Garfield of wild cats.

But Pallas's cats don't have round pupils so reputable news sites can put together listicles about the fourteen

times Pallas's cats threw more shade than Beyonce. They have them for hunting.

Generally speaking, most cats with vertical pupils are ambush hunters.

With vertical pupils, cats can control the amount of light that enters their eyes because they can expand their pupils three hundred-fold—compared to round pupils which can only expand about fifteen-fold.

Vertical pupils provide excellent vision along the y-axis and good depth perception, two things key to ambush predators. They also tend to be found on smaller hunters. Domestic cats have vertical pupils, but lions and tigers don't.

This is due to how light enters the vertical pupil. When the vertical pupils are closer to the ground, there is less blur in their vision, and the sharper the predator's vision, the more likely they are to nab dinner.

But here's where it gets weird. Cats with circular pupils are pursuit predators, meaning they chase their prey. But Pallas's cats are ambush hunters, yet they don't have the vertical slit pupils found on their relatives.

We're not entirely sure why Pallas's cats have round pupils, but the leading theory is that since Pallas's cats' territory is more varied than other small cats, ranging from deserts to plains to mountains, they need the better overall vision that round pupils provide for finding prey at different elevations and keeping an eye on their predators, like eagles.

The tradeoff is that their night vision is likely not as great as that of other cats. Because of this, they hunt mostly during the day.

Pallas's cats feed primarily on rodents like gerbils and pikas, with the occasional small bird or young marmot thrown in the mix. Their prey of choice is the pika. They're the largest animal they can consistently catch, and it's much more efficient to catch one large prey than a couple of small ones.

Pallas's cats aren't fantastic runners so their preferred hunting method is waiting and pouncing on prey as they exit their dens.

Because of their charismatic wistfulness, a common question asked about Pallas's cats is, can I own one? The answer is, as always with wild animals, no. And while Pallas's cats may resemble domestic cats, their last common ancestor lived 6.2 million years ago.

This different temperament hasn't stopped scientists from obsessing over them since at least the 1770s. They were first described by Peter Simon Pallas, who named them after himself, of course. He also gave them a polemic binomial name, *Otocolobus manul*, which means ugly-eared manul, an assessment we can't say that we agree with.

Their so-called "ugly ears" serve a purpose, however: hiding.

Unlike most other cats, which have big, pointed ears, Pallas's cats ears are short and round. This comes in handy when you spend most of your day hiding from both predators and prey, as pointy ears would be all too conspicuous. Additionally, their habitats are freezing cold in the winter, and the smaller ears expose less skin to the elements, helping them conserve heat.

Living in the steppes, their coats are also designed to blend in. In the winter their fur is grayer, and in the summer it becomes more orange-brown.

Pallas's cats may look like fat cats, but it's all fluff. Despite appearances, they are small, with the largest weighing around four and a half kilos, about the weight of an average domestic cat. Their poofy fur coat is the densest fur of any cat in the world and keeps them warm in the dead of winter.

Pallas's cats live in low densities, with only four to eight cats per hundred square kilometers. That would be like if they were here in Manhattan, there would only be three to six manuls on the entire island.

That would be nice.

Since their ranges are so huge, and since they are so solitary it makes it incredibly difficult for them to find a mate. If they do, they get pregnant for about ten weeks, after which, mom gives birth to hundred-gram kittens. They're quite possibly the cutest things we've ever seen.

Unfortunately, even after three hundred years of research, we still have much to learn about these felines. Pallas's cats are difficult to find, let alone study in the wild. Their territory is huge, they're good at hiding, and they live at low densities.

But with increasingly effective breeding programs in captivity, as well as the use of camera traps in conservation research, we're getting closer than ever to understanding the secrets behind the Pallas's cats' quizzical gaze.

Chapter 14
ECHIDNAS

The echidna is covered in thorny spines, it has a tongue half as long as its body, and a literal super power. Oh, and it lays eggs too.

Echidnas are one of the oldest living mammals on the planet. The oldest known fossil of an Echidna came from an Australian cave deposit from seventeen million years ago, during the early Miocene Era.

There are several echidna species found only in Australia and New Guinea. The most seen is the short-beaked echidna, which reigns Australia uncontested.

Echidnas, along with the platypus, are the last two surviving animals in the monotreme order. They have the strangest feature among mammals: they lay eggs. This is, of course, an evolutionary adaptation.

Just like marsupials who keep their underdeveloped young in their pouches, monotremes keep their *eggs* in their pouches. But unlike many marsupials, early monotremes found success with life in the water, and having their offspring safe from drowning in the protection of the egg proved to give them a much higher chance of survival.

Today, echidnas have found new niches to exploit and don't swim all that much. But with no evolutionary pressure to change, they've kept on with their unusual reproductive strategy.

In fact, many of their seemingly strange anatomical features were commonplace among early mammals, and we're the weird ones for not laying eggs.

If laying eggs wasn't unusual enough, the echidna's reproductive strategy gets even weirder. Males have four pronged penises, and females have two-branched reproductive tracts. This allows the male to alternate, only using two at a time to deposit his ejaculate in each of the female's tracts, while the other two rest.

To mate without hurting themselves on the female's spikes, the males have fairly long appendages, which measure about seven centimeters, and are covered in spines to help induce ovulation.

Many males will court a female simultaneously, forming a train with the dominant males up front, allowing the female multiple chances to mate successfully.

Females lay soft, leathery eggs directly into their pouches, and they hatch about ten days later.

Weirdly, the pouch is not permanent and is only formed when needed.

Their young are adorably called puggles, and when born they weigh just about two grams, about the same weight as a dollar bill. Babies need milk to survive so adult females produce through a milk patch as opposed to nipples. The babies will lap up against the milk patch on their abdomen and drink the milk that way. In the meantime, the mom will be out and about looking for food.

Also known as spiny anteaters, echidnas have received this nickname due to their diet rather than their relation to actual anteaters. Their diet is primarily made up of ants and termites, and their snouts are perfectly adapted for this tasty regimen.

Using their powerful claws to dig up prey, they'll stick their lengthy snouts into the ground, extending their long sticky tongues to catch insects, leaving the cutest little nose holes in the ground.

Their tongues are long, measuring up to eighteen centimeters, about half the length of their entire body. They don't have teeth, so echidnas "chew" their meals by pressing them against the roof of their mouths, crushing them with their powerful tongues.

Finding the ants is a little trickier, but they have one more adaptation that helps them find a meal. A sixth sense.

Their snouts are lined with electroreceptors that can detect even the slightest of muscle movements, allowing the echidnas to target their prey with razor accuracy. They can detect ants and other prey underground by the electrical signal they emit when they move. Echidnas are one of the few terrestrial animals that have this superpower.

Part of their efficacy on the hunt comes from their surprisingly large brains. Their brains have a huge prefrontal cortex. In humans, this is the part of the brain that we use for higher-level strategic thinking, which suggests they're smarter than they let on. Their brains also have a lot of folds, which is a sign of complex brain activity. Experiments have found that they are as smart as cats and rats.

Scientists have even discovered that echidnas experience rapid eye movement while sleeping. In humans REM sleep is connected with dreaming.

Echidnas are brimming with curiosities. One of the other traits that makes them unique among mammals is that their stomachs are almost devoid of acid. Since they have no stomach acid, a lot of harder materials pass straight through them–leading some scientists to believe that they have no stomachs at all, as a stomach is defined as the part of the digestive system that has acid to break down solids. This lack of acid stems from their ancestor's diet, which didn't require heavy acid to digest, and so they stopped expending energy to produce it.

The next thing on the long list of the echidna's oddities are their eyes. Their eyes are unique in the animal world because they're hard and flat. Echidnas have possibly the flattest eyes among mammals, giving them an incredibly long focal length–allowing them to spot predators from great distances. Their eyes are also hard, protecting them from getting stabbed by their spikes when they roll into a ball or are mating.

Their spikes are actually modified hairs and are primarily made of keratin. They are the echidna's first line of defense. When they're threatened, they'll go into a ball, exposing their sharp spines to ward off predators. Most times predators think better of it and back off.

They're also good at not getting spotted in the first place. Among all brushland, echidnas have good camouflage and blend in well with the ground. Their spines resemble the scraggly vegetation that they live in, making them tough for a predator to see.

Despite living near the famously scorching hot Australian outback, they don't do well in the heat. This is because they can't sweat. Lacking any sweat glands, they opt to spend the hot Australian summer days hidden away in their burrows, and the cool evenings and nights cruising for ants.

On the other hand, when it gets too cold, they can go into torpor, a temporary form of hibernation, to conserve energy. They will even do this if they can't find much food, entering torpor to save energy while they wait for more food to show up.

Echidnas have the lowest active body temperature of all mammals, at about 31-33 degrees Celsius, and during torpor, that temperature can plunge to 5 degrees Celsius.

Since they spend so much time in burrows, they've developed a high tolerance for carbon dioxide and low-oxygen environments. This is particularly useful during forest fires, as they can hide in their burrows and ride it out, so long as it doesn't get too hot.

Despite their endless list of mysteries, Echidnas are not as rare as you might expect. They have a massive range, and despite threats from invasive species and habitat destruction, their populations are waddling strong.

Chapter 15
Tawny Frogmouths

High up in Australia's tree canopy lives tawny frogmouth. It is the grumpiest, grouchiest, surliest little assassin in the world. With giant, exaggerated features, these cantankerous cranks can disappear into their surroundings, ready to strike when the moment suits them.

Frogmouths are a family of nocturnal, predatory birds related to nightjars. There are thirteen species, and they're found throughout the Indo-Pacific region, but we're focusing on one of the most emblematic species, the tawny frogmouth.

They look much like a stretched owl, but they're not closely related. It's just a case of convergent evolution, where unrelated species end up looking similar due to similar lifestyles and behaviors. But there is an important difference between them.

Owls have powerful talons for grasping and tearing at prey, but tawny frogmouths have gone another route. They have a different hunting strategy that involves their massive heads instead of their claws. Their heads are half the size of his body to accommodate a gigantic, cavernous mouth.

Unlike owls, which generally are smash-and-grab ambush predators, tawny frogmouths let their prey, primarily insects and small mammals, come to them. These birds are mimics. Their bright yellow beaks combined with little whisker-like feathers around them resemble flowers, which insects flock to. Once they fly into the tawny frogmouth's mouth, all they have to do is close it shut and swallow. This is called aggressive mimicry.

But they're not only mimics while on the hunt; they also use mimicry to blend in. They have great control over the feathers, so when roosting, they can flatten themselves out to look like a small stub that's extending off a branch.

One thing frogmouths and owls have in common is their huge eyes. They're nocturnal birds, and their gigantic eyes are meant to let in as much light as possible in low-light conditions. This helps them see incredibly well at night.

All of these features come together to give frogmouths expressive faces. Tawny frogmouths are one of the most charming birds you could meet. They look grumpy, curious, and nonchalant at the same time.

Despite their apparent bad mood, tawny frogmouths have rather adorable relationships.

They mate for life. Breeding season starts in the spring, and pairs will build their nest together.

But tawny frogmouths aren't good at building nests, and males tend to toss a bunch of sticks together and call it a day.

Males and females share parental roles, and they take turns incubating the eggs. Food is also provided by both parents until the fledglings are

ready to leave the nest at about five weeks of age.

Tawny frogmouths have a vast range and thrive across mainland Australia and Tasmania. They prefer regions with lots of trees, but they have been seen in deserts as well. Because of their adaptability, tawny frogmouth populations are stable. While they face threats from habitat destruction, bushfires, and insecticides, these grumpy little assassins are resilient.

Chapter 16
Wombats

Wombats are the heroes of the bushfires, the stealer of hearts, and the knights of the most adorable joust in the world.

Wombats are a family of marsupials closely related to koalas. Only found in Australia, there are three living species of wombat. The common wombat is the most prolific, and are found in southeastern Australia, as well as Tasmania. The other two species are its less handsome cousins, the Northern and Southern hairy-nosed wombat, which are primarily found in Queensland and South Australia, respectively.

The hairy-nosed wombats look like someone had to draw a wombat from memory but got confused halfway through and drew a possum instead.

Wombats are famous for their chill attitudes, spending three to eight hours a day eating.

But despite their reputation, in wombat country, things can get spicy.

For male wombats, territory is everything, and when a male challenges another for his land, they go to war. The two males slam into each other like knights in the joust, or more aptly, like two stuffed animals being smashed together. They snap and claw at one another, using their heavy bodies to try and knock the other to the ground. This is mortal wombat.

In the end, size is king, and the largest male usually wins. In a final message of their distaste for one another, they both scrape the ground with their front legs. In the wombat world, this is akin to a death threat.

While it may be hard to tell from seeing pictures of wombats, these cuties can be large. They can reach up to one meter in length and weigh up to thirty kilograms. They're sturdy and muscular animals, despite how round they might look.

And they put that muscle to good use. While they may look pudgy, they can run fast, as fast as the fastest human alive, for up to a minute.

Wombats are herbivores, and they hover up everything in front of them, from shrubs to roots to bushes. These are all low-calorie foods, so they're not likely to put on much fat but they can build lots of muscle.

Since their diet is made of vast quantities of hard plant matter, their teeth are constantly being worn down, so wombats have developed rodent-like incisors that never stop growing. This is yet another great example of convergent evolution, as wombats are not closely related to beavers, but they both share the same adaptations with their similar diets.

While it's hard to imagine these wombats ever taking a break from munching away, they can survive several days without eating. They have a slow metabolism, and it can take them up to two weeks to digest a meal. This can be a helpful tool when they're trapped in the burrows, either by a predator or by bushfire.

Wombats are nocturnal and they don't have great vision so instead they rely on their big leathery noses to find exactly what they're looking for: low-lying plant matter. Then they dig for it. They're excellent burrowers thanks to their large and powerful claws. Wombats are natural excavators.

Wombats' potent front legs and strong claws help them dig through just about anything. While you might think that when they dig, some dirt would end up in their marsupial pouches, they have evolved to have backward-opening pouches, which prevent any dirt from griming up their joeys.

All that digging has led to some pretty impressive burrows. They are massive, can be up to twenty meters long, and have over fifteen entrances. All the holes to the burrows connect underground. They're so well built that other animals seek them out for shelter. The marsupial architect, the wombat!

Wombats are considered the heroes of the bushfire season in Australia because they're reported to share their burrows with so many species of animals. But sharing isn't the right word for it. You could say that a lot of animals squat in their burrows during the fires. That would be a little more accurate.

Wombats usually live in the same burrow their entire lives unless they're forced to leave it. Several wombats can live in the same burrow, provided it's large enough. These burrows make effective hideouts from predators, but a burrow with an open door doesn't make a safehouse. So wombats have developed their own versions of blast doors: their butts.

They have a flat behind. That's because they have an inch-thick cartilage plate that covers their entire pelvis, and it acts like a shield. To escape predation, they'll dig in and leave their butt hanging out; their butt is so well protected that nothing can get through that. Even a tassie devil would have a hard time pulling it out by that huge cartilage plate.

But even more so than their rump plates, the most famous thing about wombats is what they leave behind: their poo. Their feces are unique in the animal kingdom because they're cubed. That's right, wombats have dice-shaped poo.

This is thought to be a communication strategy, as it allows them to stack their poo to mark their territory without fear of their unique droppings rolling away.

Eating as much as they do, wombats can poop up to a hundred cubes a day. Yet despite this prolific contribution to science, the mechanics behind their production are still a mystery to us. Scientists have discovered that their stool only solidifies in the last bit of the intestine. Their intestines contain parts that are stretchy and parts that are solid, but how it all comes together to produce cubes is still unknown.

Scientists and engineers are still looking at the problem because it's a novel way of making cubes, which could potentially be applied in production chains around the world.

When wombats aren't eating, fighting, or pooping, they're mating. Mating can happen at any time throughout the year, though it's most common during the rainy season.

Unlike other marsupials, which give birth to multiple joeys that need to compete to survive, wombats only give birth to a single joey. Born about the size of one of their poop cubes, it won't be for another six months until they're ready to leave the pouch. Once they start growing hair, they go from alien-looking to incredibly cute.

By fifteen months, they'll be fully weaned and ready to fend for themselves. They will stick close to Mom for another few months, as it's dangerous to go alone.

Because of how much time is expended raising just one joey–each mother raises one joey every two years–it's actually difficult to recover their population if it were to decline. While the common wombat is thriving, its cousins aren't having nearly as much success. The northern hairy-nosed wombat is critically endangered, with only eighty mature adults left in the wild, living in a single colony in Queensland.

The southern hairy-nosed wombat is faring better than their northern brethren, but is listed as near-threatened.

Fortunately, due to conservation efforts and protection from invasive species, the northern hairy-nosed wombats have been steadily increasing in numbers, and they are now at their largest population size since European colonization.

With any luck, this trend will continue, and all three species of wombat will begin to thrive. The world needs more chunky, fuzzy lawnmowers with a serious attitude–or, at least, I do.

Chapter 17
BANDICOOTS

Bandicoots are the survivors of extinction, the earthworm's bane, and the inspiration for one of the most beloved video game characters of all time.

Found across mainland Australia, Tasmania, and New Guinea, there are around twenty bandicoot species, and they thrive in all sorts of terrain, from the outback to rainforests to woodlands and swamps. They range in size from tiny—the golden bandicoot, which weighs just three hundred grams—to relatively large—the northern brown bandicoot, which weighs ten times as their smallest cousins.

But we're focusing on one of the great conservation stories of the past decade: the eastern barred bandicoot.

They belong to the long-nosed branch of the bandicoot family and are distinguished by the cute little stripes on their butts.

The other half of the true bandicoot family are the short-nosed bandicoots, which, as their name suggests, have short snouts. Outside the family of true bandicoots, the Peramelidae family, there are a few species commonly referred to as bandicoots despite belonging to different families.

Included are the rabbit-eared bandicoots or bilbies. These are distinct from true bandicoots in that they have large, rabbit-like ears, long hind legs, bushy tails, and a particular resistance to powerful rings.

But the weirdest-looking bandicoot, which isn't a bandicoot, is the pig-footed bandicoot.

These cuties had long legs along with hoof-like feet, and they reportedly would gallop around like a horse. Unfortunately, they are likely extinct, as the last sighting was in the 1920s.

Both species split from true bandicoots in the late Oligocene or early Miocene, and in 2014, a new genus was described, titled simply "crash," or crash bandicoot.

This cheekily named, newly discovered extinct species, is one of the earliest found relatives of the modern bandicoots after they split from bilbies and their pig-footed cousins.

Bandicoots are nocturnal predators. With their long noses, they excel at sniffing out and digging up worms. They use their small front legs to dig perfectly snout-sized holes. Their snouts are lined with highly sensitive nerves that help them detect the movements of prey underground.

They're not exclusively carnivorous and will eat anything they can get their snouts around, including crickets, roots, and if they're desperate–scorpions.

While real bandicoots don't spend their time collecting video game points, one thing the game did get right is their wonky run. The reason for this is their long hind legs, which resemble kangaroo legs, and allow them to escape predators quickly.

Bandicoots are solitary species, only ever meeting up to mate. Living up to three years in the wild, they have short pregnancies at just twelve days. This is one of the shortest pregnancies in the mammal world.

Not all bandicoots are lucky enough to make it to old age. Due to their small size, they make easy prey for predators like dingoes and eagles. Though more recently they've had the misfortune of being preyed upon by introduced species like dogs, feral cats, and foxes.

Once found extensively across Southern Australia, eastern barred bandicoots have been driven to extinction on the mainland, and until recently could only be found in Tasmania, where there are fewer foxes.

A few adults were released on a nearby island just off the coast and let that population try to proliferate for a few years. Then some of them were brought over to the mainland. In the past five years they've gone from less than a hundred to about three hundred.

In some areas, like Phillip Island, conservation projects primarily focused on increasing little penguin populations, but their banning of dogs and outdoor cats and eradication of foxes has inadvertently led to a boom for many species, including the eastern barred bandicoot.

As reintroduction programs gain traction and efforts to eradicate invasive species succeed, hopefully we'll soon see a return of the coolest, denim clad, polar-bear-riding marsupial to the mainland.

Chapter 18
PLATYPUS

The platypus is a freshwater chimaera. Its unique biology confused scientists for decades. They're found in wetlands across the east and southeast coast of Australia and throughout Tasmania. The platypus is one of two members of the monotreme order, the other being the echidna, which was mentioned in an earlier chapter.

They're smaller than you might think–only measuring about fifty centimeters long, but their small frame packs one of the most peculiar sets of adaptations in the animal kingdom.

Unlike placental mammals and marsupials, which both give birth to live young, monotremes are mammals that lay eggs. But laying eggs is by far one of the least interesting things about the platypus. These cuties bring it in every category of being weird to the point where, frankly, it's hard to keep track of.

The platypus is a perfect example of convergent evolution, when similar traits evolve separately in different species based on similar problems the species had to solve. For example, flying squirrels in

North America are not at all related to Australia's sugar gliders, but they both have evolved the same means of transport. But instead of evolving one or two traits similar to other species, the platypus is seemingly made up entirely of parts from other animals.

The platypus has a bill like a duck, a tail like a beaver, webbed feet like an otter, electroreceptors like a shark, limbs on their sides like a reptile, and venom like a viper. They also lay eggs like a turtle, and lack a stomach and teeth like an echidna.

The platypus looks like what happens when evolution hits the shuffle button, but this couldn't be further from the truth. While their variety of parts makes them look like a freshwater chimaera, all of their disparate features come together perfectly to create the ultimate mashup, resulting in one highly effective weirdo.

When British explorers first brought a specimen of a platypus back from Australia to England it was deemed too ridiculous to be real no one could believe that this creature wasn't just a Frankenstein of a bunch of different animals stitched together so it took several more expeditions and more specimens to prove that this thing was indeed a mammal that laid eggs with a duck-like bill.

Each one of their strange features serves a valuable purpose. First up, their bill. The reason platypuses have evolved to have a duck-like bill is because of the environment that they were able to conquer—rivers, lakes, and wetlands. Fresh water is murky, and if you're going to hunt in it, you need to rely on something other than your eyes.

And so, the platypus has evolved a superpower: electroreception. Platypuses don't have good eyesight but they see the world through electric pulses.

Commonly found in sharks, rays, and few other fish species, platypus have bills lined with tiny dots called electroreceptors. Whenever you move a muscle, the contraction generates an electric field. The platypus uses the electroreceptors in the skin of their bills

to calculate the voltage difference around them, allowing them to target the electric fields of moving prey with pinpoint accuracy.

The platypus dives, heading for the bottom, shaking its head quickly from side to side, seeking out any moving prey. If he detects anything, he can use his sixth sense to zoom in and focus on the prey.

But their sixth sense isn't the only trick up their sleeves; their bills are also sensitive. They can detect even the slightest of touches. Their beaks are incredibly sensitive and capable of sensing all kinds of little waves and changes in the water pressure.

All of this makes the platypus's bill the perfect sensory organ for hunting prey in the dark and murky fresh water. They're so effective that they hunt with their eyes closed.

They spend about 40 percent of the night actively looking for food, so they need to be well-equipped.

While bills are great for housing large numbers of electroreceptors, they are also perfect for their feeding strategy. Their bill allows them to bite into the muck and push out any excess mud and water before swallowing.

One consequence of the development of electroreceptors is that adult platypuses have no teeth. In order to crunch up their meals, they scoop up small rocks and press them against the top of their bills.

Platypuses also lack stomachs. Just like echidnas, their food is digested by going straight from the esophagus to the intestine. Their lack of stomach is so ancient that the part of the mammalian DNA in charge of making a stomach and the digestive compounds in it is entirely gone.

Borrowing yet another strategy, but this time from crocodiles, on top of the platypus's bill are two nostrils. This positioning allows them to stick a little of their snout and just the tops of the torso out of the water to breathe without giving away their position to predators. When they dive, they close their nostrils.

Platypuses only dive for about thirty seconds at a time, so it's not long before they have to resurface again. Generally they need between ten and twenty seconds of recovery time before they can dive down again.

The second most iconic thing about the platypus is their wide tail–an adaptation that they share with a species on the other side of the world–the beaver. These tails are perfectly evolved for life in the water, offering the platypus both excellent propulsion and steering. But they also have a surprising use–carrying things.

These tails are dexterous, and they use them to carry reeds and sticks to construct their burrows. When they're pressing sticks to their backs with their tails, they look like they have on the cutest little backpacks. Then, they will use these reeds and sticks to barricade the entrance to their homes, allowing them to snooze in peace.

The entrance to their den is usually underwater, but can extend up the bank up to five meters. They can spend about twenty hours a day there and come out to go hunting.

Next we have the platypus's rather unusual feet. They resemble otter feet in that they are heavily webbed, but the closer you look, the weirder they get. Their webbing extends well beyond the tips of their fingers, leading to their claws being in a strange place—halfway up their feet. This offers a good compromise for both digging and swimming.

Their feet are similar to scuba fins, as the webbing extends beyond where the actual bone is. This allows them to be much larger than they would be if the webbing stopped at the fingertips, as it does in most webbed-footed species.

Spending much of their time floating around looking for food, you may have noticed something strange about their legs—they're located on the sides of their body rather than underneath them. This is strange in the mammalian world and is usually only seen in reptiles. This adaptation makes them more hydrodynamic, a must for an aquatic mammal.

They don't come on land often, but when they do, it's adorable. These small, stumpy limbs offer them little support on land, though they get the job done when needed.

But beyond strange webbing, male platypuses have an extra weird adaptation on their hind limbs: they have sharp spurs. Sharp, venomous spurs. Male platypuses use their venom primarily during the mating season in combat with other male platypuses. Interestingly, the venom, while it does share chemical properties and effects with reptile venom, is not meant to kill or even permanently damage tissue. Platypus venom is meant to subdue competing males while they mate with prospective females.

While it may seem strange for a mammal to have venom, they're not the only ones that do; some shrews have it too! Venom used to be more commonplace in the mammalian world, and platypuses, being an old lineage, feature a lot of adaptations that while seem strange to us, were quite common back in the day.

Once the battle for mating rights is won, females will dig out their burrows in preparation for their young. After four weeks of gestation, two to three eggs are laid and will hatch after about ten days.

Since the mom has no teats, the young, called puggles, will lap up milk from her mammary glands for about four months before they're old enough to eat solid meals.

Unfortunately, they're extremely sensitive to the health of their environment and, if there's a lot of pollution in their lakes and river systems, they get rapidly affected. This has been decreasing their survival rates.

The platypus is listed as a near-threatened species and with their numbers decreasing, it will take a concerted effort from all of us to maintain the wetlands they call home.

The world needs more weirdos, and weirdos with painful, venomous spurs aren't the weirdos you want to piss off by destroying their homes.

Chapter 19
HOGNOSES

The hognose snake is so cute and derpy. This isn't a nope rope, this is a string king. At first sight, you might think that this little guy is harmless, and you would be 100 percent right. Unless you're a frog. In that case this handsome jawline will be the last thing you see. Watch out, Kermit!

Hognoses are relatively short snakes spread among three genera: one from North America, one from South America, and one from Madagascar. The three genera are not closely related, but they all have convergently evolved to be amazing diggers by making use of the most unusual of shovels: their faces.

The first of the three hognoses is the North American genus *Heterodon*. They live in the plains east of the Rockies, from central Canada to northern Mexico.

Their genus name *Heterodon* means "different tooth," as these snakes have unusual teeth. Most snakes have fangs at the front of their face, but hognoses have their fangs situated farther into their mouths, more toward their throat; so if they are trying to go for a

frog or a salamander, which is a little more viscous or even slimy, it helps secure their prey in their mouths and keep them from escaping.

Most venomous snakes, like vipers, have highly developed venom-injecting fangs at the front of their mouths. Their strategy is to kill their prey quickly and then swallow.

Rear-fanged snakes, like hognoses, generally aren't venomous so they need a series of backward-facing teeth to grasp their prey and move it toward their throat and into their bellies.

In a way, this kind of snake is the only one that chews.

These guys are not venomous to humans or other large mammals. Since they're harmless to predators, they've evolved to resemble rattlesnakes. This is a form of Batesian mimicry, where a harmless prey species mimics a dangerous species to deter predators.

This might trick predators, but if you encounter one in the wild, you can tell them apart by their adorable pug-like faces.

These faces are, of course, an evolutionary adaptation. All snakes have a terminal scale in their face, and in hognoses, it's hardened and shovel-shaped. They use it to dig in the ground.

Hognoses live in areas with gravelly or sandy soil, the ideal habitat for digging. When looking for a safe place to hide, they move their face from side to side, while making undulating movements with their body, quickly burrowing into the ground.

Digging helps them hide from predators, as well as take cover from the brutal sun in the prairies. It also gives them a safe place to lay their eggs. And most importantly, their favorite prey are other burrowing animals like toads and lizards.

Hognoses take the hunt underground. Toads often puff themselves to make themselves harder to eat, but hognoses use their rear fangs to pop them like a balloon.

Unfortunately, despite resembling venomous snakes, these are dangerless noodles. But they have another line of defense— the power of *acting*. North American Hognoses, particularly the Eastern Hognose, are known to raise their head and flatten it when threatened. This gives them a menacing look similar to a cobra.

Because of this, people call them "puff adders," the name of an unrelated venomous viper species from Africa.

Hognoses will hiss and strike but not bite. At worst they'll headbutt their aggressor, though this is more likely to give them a concussion than to hurt the predator. And if that doesn't work, they go full ham.

They're experts in thanatosis, which means they like to play dead, or rather, they play *dying*. They start by putting on a hell of a show, excreting all their smelly bodily fluids, peeing and pooping all over the place and squirming like they're in the worst pain possible. If that doesn't scare their predators away, their last-ditch attempt is to lie motionless.

The plan is to make the predator think that the snake is sick or rotten, making it lose interest. This doesn't always work and

predatory birds, like hawks and owls, seem to not be bothered by it. A meal's a meal.

The Malagasy and South American hognoses are thought to exhibit similar behaviors, but unfortunately haven't been studied enough. If you're thinking of going into herpetology, consider studying them so we can talk about them.

Chapter 20
Glow Worms

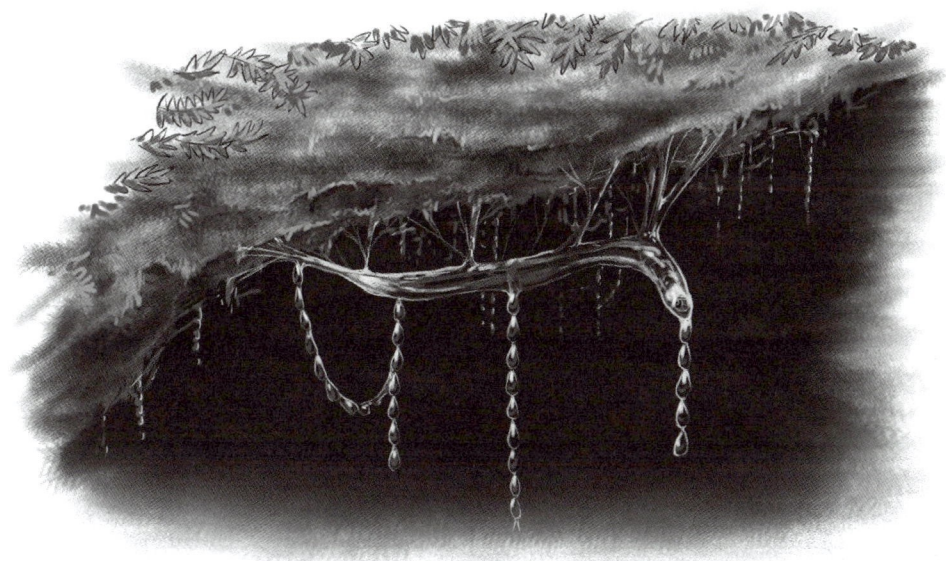

Glow worms are the deadly sirens of Australia. They're one of the most mesmerizing animals on Earth. Inconspicuous under sunlight, at night they get together to form living constellations so beautiful that prey can't resist.

Despite their name and appearance, glow worms are more closely related to a house fly than to a worm. They're actually baby insects. They're the larvae of a fly species called the fungus gnat. These glow worms are to fungus gnats what caterpillars are to butterflies.

Some bioluminescent beetles are sometimes also called glow worms, but in Australia, glow worms refer to gnats of the genus *Arachnocampa*.

There are nine recognized species in this genus. One of them lives in New Zealand, another one in Tasmania, and the remaining seven in mainland Australia. The glow worms in the drawing are from the Great Otway National Park and are aptly named *Arachnocampa otwayensis*. Their name means the spider worm from the *otway*. They don't have eight legs, but they have a similar hunting strategy.

Their glow comes from strands of mucus. A single larva can put up to seventy strands, which can be up to forty centimeters long in some cases. These sticky strands emit light that we humans perceive to be blue. Flying insects and other small animals get attracted to the light and get snared in the mucus. The glow worm then descends from its nest and consumes its prey, just like a spider in a spider web.

Their most common prey are midges, though mosquitoes and moths are often consumed.

This might seem like an overcomplicated way of hunting, but it's surprisingly effective, and a single colony might contain tens of thousands of individuals. The only tradeoff is that they can only live in areas with no wind as it would tangle the strands. That's why they're mostly found in caves or deep in dense forests.

Their bioluminescence is the result of a chemical reaction. A luciferase enzyme acts on a protein molecule called luciferin. Their name might sound familiar because they come from the word Lucifer, which means light-giver.

And light they give for almost their whole life. The larval stage of the fungus gnat might last for up to a year. Then they pupate for about a week.

Female pupae are brighter than male pupae and are thought to attract adult males, who wait for the females to emerge from their pupae to mate with them. You would be tempted to tell the males to chill and let them be, but their adult life only lasts about a week, so there's no time to wait.

After seven days of mating, the female lays about a hundred eggs and dies. Males die shortly after as they cannot feed.

Since light is a necessary part of their life, they have evolved a lot of ways to control it. They can manage the intensity and emit more light when the time is right to catch prey. If they feel vibrations in their snares, they will glow brighter. If they're exposed to light, they will switch themselves off.

They're also known to observe each other and synchronise their glow cycles, though we're still not sure why.

There's so much we still don't know about these beautiful hunters, but we're starting to see the light.

Chapter 21
Elephant and Harbour Seals

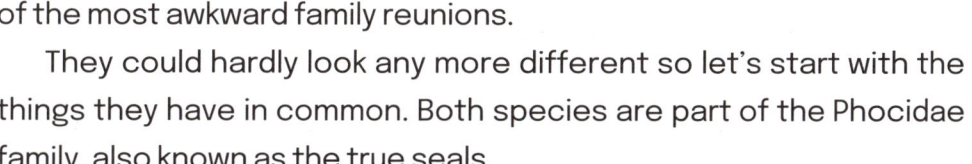

Elephant seals are wonderful weirdos that wouldn't be out of place in a *Star Wars* movie. Their appearance is even more striking when contrasted with their closest relatives, the harbour seals, which are basically Disney characters come to life. They are the hosts of the most awkward family reunions.

They could hardly look any more different so let's start with the things they have in common. Both species are part of the Phocidae family, also known as the true seals.

These chunky guys' biology is geared for life in water. To reduce drag when diving, they have backward-facing hind flippers and lack external ears.

The drawback is that it also makes it harder for them to walk on land. They have to drag themselves across the rocks to move around.

Their distant cousins, the sea lions, have similar lifestyles, but their sideways-pointing legs help them walk on land more gracefully.

Let's look at their many differences. First, their size disparity. Elephant seals are the largest seals in the world, while harbour seals are one of the smallest.

The local northern elephant seal bulls can weigh up to three tons and measure five meters in length—the same dimensions as an SUV.

Females are smaller at three meters in length and a maximum weight of one ton.

Harbour seals are miniscule in comparison. At about 150 kilograms, for the largest males, they're a twentieth of the size of an elephant seal. Females are a little smaller than the males, but they're not quite as sexually dimorphic as their gigantic cousins.

Despite looking like cute water puppies, harbour seals can't claim the title of smallest seal in the world. That distinction goes to adorable Baikal seals, which are half as big as harbour seals. These Siberian cuties are also the only seals to live exclusively in freshwater.

It's time to address the elephant in the room. Hey, elephant seal, why the long face?

The male elephant seal's proboscis is the Swiss knife of animal appendages. They make them look like overweight water saigas, but they're incredibly useful.

They're secondary sexual characteristics, with the largest, strongest males usually having the larger trunks. So, if you're a male you don't want to challenge another male that has a bigger schnozz. This generally prevents injuries as it cuts down on unnecessary fights.

They have cavities inside the proboscis that act as resonators when they roar, making elephant seals some of the loudest mammals on Earth.

The least obvious, but perhaps most important, feature of the proboscis is its ability to catch moisture from the air. During the breeding season males can go up to three months without eating. Since they get most of their water from their food, it also means they can get dehydrated over time. So, being able to trap moisture in their proboscis is lifesaving.

Their breeding period is already dangerous enough. In January, they look for ideal breeding spots and fight each other for the best real estate. The fights are ridiculous, with massive mammals full of blubber biting and pushing each other until one gives up.

A few weeks later the females show up and choose the male with the best breeding grounds. A big successful male with a nice, comfortable property, can have a harem of up to fifty females. And in some extreme cases, they can reach triple digits. That means that in a lifetime a big male can sire over five hundred pups.

Females are much smaller, sometimes just a tenth of the male's size, making elephant seals the most sexually dimorphic mammals on Earth. They don't have a proboscis as they don't fast nearly as long as the males and can go back to water soon after giving birth, leaving the pups to fend for themselves.

Luckily for the pups, elephant seal milk is about 50 percent fat, so they get lots of calories and grow quickly. For context, deliciously thick cow milk is only about 3.5 percent fat.

Despite the whole harem thing, female elephant seals are independent ladies. They're loyal to the land, not to the man. Males who don't have territories will try to sneak into other males' land and mate with the females. So, the big male spends most of his time chasing away younger opportunistic males and little time copulating.

That's what they don't tell you about elephant seal harem ownership: the upkeep is a full-time job.

Harbour seals are more private about their breeding. Courtship and copulation take place underwater, so nobody knows exactly how

it happens. All we know is that early in the summer females come out and give birth to well-developed pups.

They nurse for three to four weeks and then are ready to go into the water. Zero drama.

Feeding strategies are also affected by size. Tiny harbour seals like relatively shallow waters like estuaries, and even rivers, where they can catch fish like salmon and shad.

Female elephant seals go to more pelagic hunting grounds, while males can catch prey at the bottom of the ocean at depths of over 1,500 meters. Lanternfish and squid are their most common deepwater prey.

Mammals are not meant to go so deep, and so the northern elephant seal has a few adaptations to deal with deep water. The main one is the ability to store huge amounts of oxygen in their body.

They're the only animals known to store oxygenated red blood cells in their spleen, which then get gradually released into their bloodstream.

Extra oxygen is also stored in their muscles and their blood, as they have high concentrations of oxygen-binding proteins. On top of that they can slow down their heartbeat and their metabolism. All of this helps them hold their breath for up to a hundred minutes, the longest of any mammals outside cetaceans.

Harbour seals can hold their breath for a more modest, but still amazing, thirty minutes. When they're hunting they have to be careful not to become prey themselves. Despite their size difference, elephant seals and harbour seals have the same main predators: great white sharks and killer whales.

And yet, despite their formidable predators, they're thriving.

Both species are protected, and their numbers have been growing steadily over the past few decades.

If you want to meet the giant that Luke Skywalker milked in that movie, this is probably the closest thing to that on Earth.

Chapter 22

Japanese Spider Crab

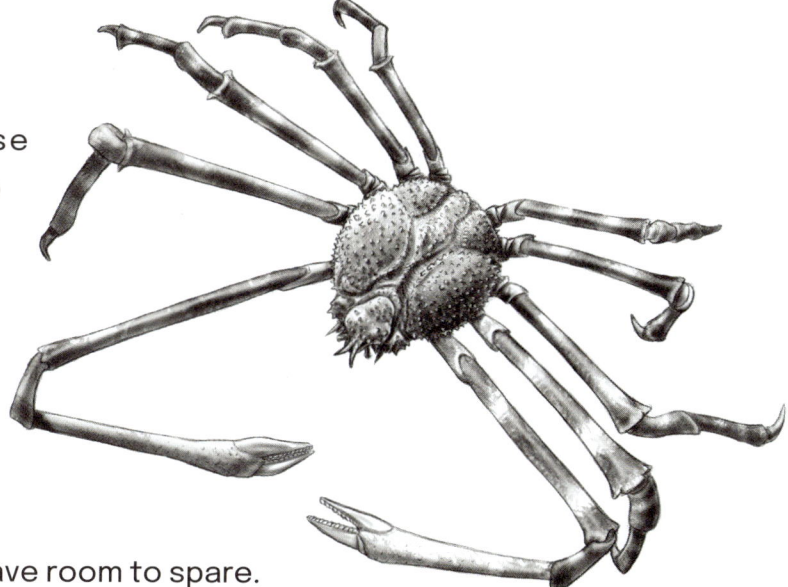

The Japanese spider crab is the closest thing on Earth to facehuggers, except this guy could hug your entire family at the same time and have room to spare. They're the reason Godzilla got scared and left the sea. They're the largest crustacean in the world.

The Japanese spider crabs, or *Macrocheira kaempferi,* are part of the Inachidae family. They're not actually spiders. Their name comes from the unusually long limbs that make them look like the daddy longlegs of the ocean.

Among their closest living relatives are the slightly smaller common spider crabs, which can be about three centimeters long– over a hundred times smaller than their real-life kaiju cousin.

They're tiny little goobers compared to the mighty Japanese spider crabs, which can have a total wingspan of about 3.7 meters. They dwarf every other crustacean in the world. Even the coconut crabs are tiny in comparison.

Their carapace is comparatively small, at about forty centimeters, but it all adds up to a hefty twenty kilograms.

They're a type of decorator crab and furbish their carapaces and legs with plant matter, as well as sponges, anemones, and other ocean organisms, which continue growing on the crab's back. This helps camouflage on the ocean floor and avoid predators, especially when they're young.

When they're small, their long, decorated legs look like seaweed stalks. But as they get bigger, protection from predators becomes less important, but they maintain their lumpy carapace, which, in deep water with dim lighting, looks like a rock.

They're omnivores, but they prefer eating plants and carrion instead of hunting. They're gentle giants.

Like most crustaceans they come into this world invisible to the eye. Their journey to humongousness begins as microscopic eggs. Japanese spider crab reproduction begins when the male uses his claws to deposit a sperm packet into the female. She carries the eggs until they hatch about ten days later into plankton.

The eggs are so tiny that in a single season a female can lay over a million eggs. Unfortunately, the odds are stacked against them and only a handful reach adulthood. To get there they'll need to go through four stages of development. The speed of their growth depends on food availability and water temperature.

Like other invertebrates, they keep growing throughout their life. Their lifespan is thought to be about a hundred years, so there's plenty of time to get huge.

When they moult they become immobile, and they emerge from the rear of their carapace. In larger individuals this process can take almost two hours.

Unfortunately, fewer and fewer of these crabs are getting the chance to become centenarians. Trawling fisheries sweep the ocean floor, taking everything with them. In some regions spider crab legs are sought after, and the demand has affected populations. The current average size of Japanese spider crabs captured in some areas is just over a meter.

We don't know their current conservation status because deepwater species populations are difficult to evaluate, but there are efforts to help these leggy redheads.

It's now illegal to catch them in the winter when they travel to shallower waters to mate. There's also a restocking program using larvae hatched in artificial ponds.

This is possible because they grow well in pools, ponds, and aquaria. They seem happy, provided they have enough room and food, and the water is the right temperature—about 10 degrees Celsius.

With populations declining and a preference for deep water, your best chance to see them is at an aquarium. We don't always recommend going to places that keep animals in captivity, but some facilities do great conservation and education work.

So, if you can, see a Japanese spider crab in person. It's one of the most amazing animals you'll ever see.

Chapter 23
Banana Slugs

Banana slugs! They're delicious and full of potassium. Oh, wait, never mind. They're gastropods. Slimy yellow gastropods that are adorable, spotty, sticky, and...did I already say slimy? They're slimy!

Banana slugs are North American terrestrial slugs in the genus *Ariolimax*. Species include the California banana slug, the Pacific banana slug, and the slender banana slug. But why are they called banana slugs? The answer may surprise you. Just kidding; it's because they look like bananas.

Banana slugs come in a variety of colours, from bright yellow to green, brown, tan, even white!

Some have so many dark spots that they appear black.

You can find banana slugs on forest floors along North America's Pacific Coast. The perfect forest for a banana slug is moist, cool, and densely packed with coniferous trees like California Redwoods and Douglas Firs.

An average banana slug may only measure seven inches or eighteen centimeters, but the big boys can measure well over

twenty centimeters in length, which makes them the second largest terrestrial slug in the world.

If you're thinking bigger means faster, think again. Banana slugs can only cover fifteen centimeters per minute. That's nine meters every hour, which makes these gastropods one of the slowest animals on Earth.

They have two sets of tentacles: the ocular tentacles on top, which carry the eyes, and the sensory tentacles just below that, which they use to taste and smell potential food.

This fleshy part at the front of the slug is called the mantle. It serves to protect the genital and anal pores, which are higher on the slug than you might expect.

Banana slugs have not one but two ways to breathe: gas exchange through their mucus membrane covering their entire body, and through a little hole on their right side. It's called a pneumostone and it can expand and contract to allow air in, which allows the slug to breathe through its single lung.

All the way around the bottom of the slug is a cute little frilly line. It's called the skirt, and it consists of muscle bands that help to pull it along the ground. And that's how it moves.

Once it finds food, it has to eat it. Have you ever wondered what's inside a slug's mouth? The answer is a radula. It's like a sharp rasp tongue covered in rows of about 27,000 microscopic teeth, continually breaking off and being replaced by new rows.

Banana slugs are mostly herbivores. They'll eat plants, leaves, stems, seeds, spores, flowers, fungi, and fruit. They'll also dine on feces and animal carcasses. Not exactly a picky eater.

After the slug processes its food, it recycles the nutrients back into the soil.

Banana slugs are mostly out and about at night or on cool, moist days. With no shell to hide in, they are always in danger of drying up.

Luckily, they're equipped with slime. This thick, sticky mucus helps the slug keep hydrated. Mucus granules emerge from the slug's skin cells, then pop open and absorb nearby water and nutrients. One mucus granule can absorb a hundred times its own volume.

The mucus also helps them move, working as a sort of lubricant that allows them to glide smoothly over the rough terrain of the forest floor. And it acts as an adhesive to stick to steep surfaces and even hang upside down from their slime threads. Spider slug!

Slime is also the banana slug's greatest defense against hungry predators. This slug is targeted by all kinds of animals, including small mammals, snakes, salamanders, birds, and shrews. When they're attacked, they produce extra slime, which contains an anesthetic that can numb the predator's mouth and create a foul taste.

Some animals have gotten around this. Some raccoons have figured out that if they coat the slugs in dirt, it'll make them easier to go down. Other predators have yet to master eating banana slugs. For example, snakes have been found with their mouths glued shut with mucus.

There's an old myth that says picking up or kissing a slug will bring you good fortune. But you should never do this. Their coat of slime helps them with breathing and protection, so your sweaty and dirty hands can hurt them.

Slime is also helpful when it comes time to reproduce. As banana slugs move slowly through the forest, they leave slime trails, which give off pheromones that other sexy slugs can follow.

If two slugs like each other, they impregnate each other. Like many other mollusks, banana slugs are hermaphrodites, which means this banana slug can mate with any other banana slug. Talk about equal rights!

When they meet, the slug lovers will court each other by swiping their tails, nipping, and lunging. Other mating rituals include eating each other's slime and wrapping themselves in a sort of nuptial bed of slime.

When unfurled, the male phallus can stretch the slug's full body length. So that allows for mating between slugs of slightly different sizes.

Banana slugs will lay twenty to thirty small eggs, which spend the winter in the ground and hatch the following spring. Baby slugs will leave the nest to find their own territory that offers food and shelter, and will make the land a slimier and more colourful place.

Chapter 24
Mudskippers

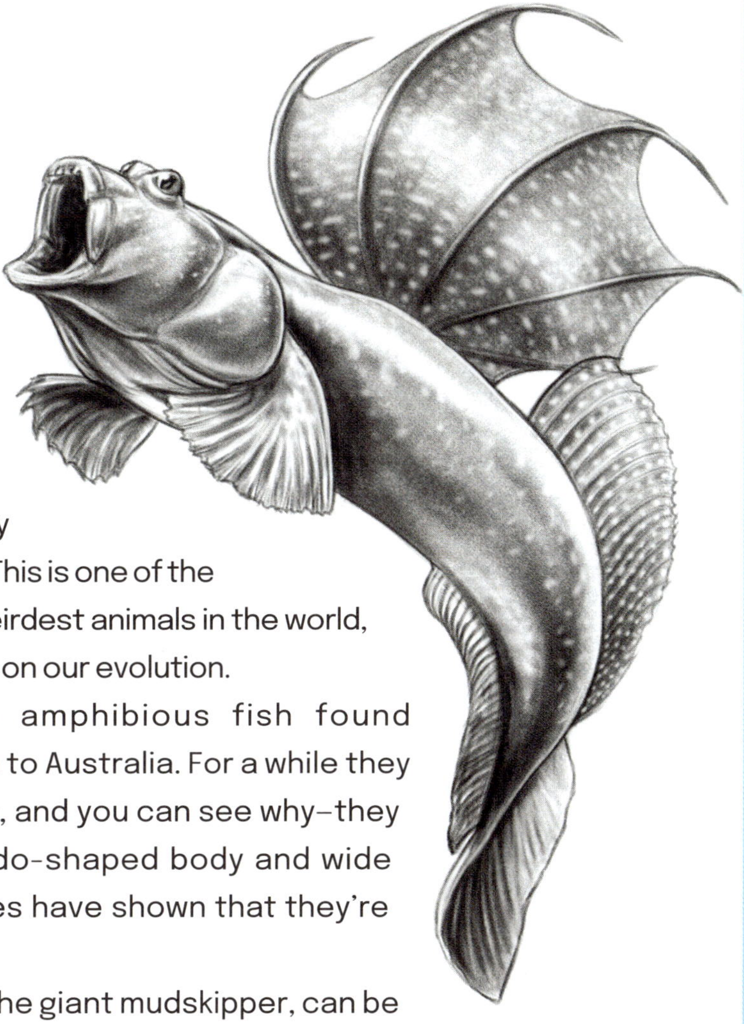

The mudskipper is a fish that lives primarily on land. They use water bubbles like a tongue to catch prey, they shovel mud with their mouths, and they have some seriously epic and floppy battles. This is one of the most fascinating and weirdest animals in the world, and one that sheds light on our evolution.

Mudskippers are amphibious fish found extensively from Africa to Australia. For a while they were in the goby family, and you can see why–they have the same torpedo-shaped body and wide face. But recent studies have shown that they're their own family.

Some species, like the giant mudskipper, can be up to thirty centimeters long, but most species are about ten centimeters long.

Mudskippers live in swamps, estuaries, and other intertidal ecosystems. But while most other fish there are active during high tide, mudskippers dine when the tide is low. Also unlike other fish, they dine on land.

Their entire strategy consists of walking or skipping in the mud, looking for insects and other small animals to eat. They're just one of the few fish families able to breathe out of the water.

Bichirs and lungfish are some of the other fish that you might find plodding about in the mud.

Of course, fish hunting in the mud requires a specialized breathing system. Like frogs, mudskippers can take oxygen from the air through their skin and the soft tissue in their mouths and throats. This is called cutaneous respiration.

The only caveat is that they must be wet for it to work. They're like reverse gremlins and their permanent need for moisture is the only reason they haven't taken over the world.

This is why they like mud so much. They need frequent access to water which they get from the tidal pools formed in the mud.

Besides breathing through their skin, they also keep oxygenated water and air in their gills. This is used as a backup in case they start drying out.

Walking on land requires a completely different form of locomotion than swimming. Thankfully, mudskippers have muscular pectoral fins. For these guys, it's "water out, guns out."

The joint between the radials and the fin rays is functionally an elbow. The radial also connects to the body at an articulated joint that is their shoulder. And all of this is supported by powerful muscles that make them great at pushups and at hopping around.

They can move one fin at a time, like we walk, or they can move them forward at the same time, in a move called "crutching." Some species can even climb branches and tree trunks, using their concave hip bones as a sort of sucker for extra grip.

Being terrestrial hunters, they need good eyesight to find their prey. Their eyes have evolved to work better outside of the water than

in it. They sit at the top of their head and can move independently and with a huge range of motion, giving them almost a 360-degree field of vision.

Their only problem is that they only work well when moist. To deal with this problem, their eyes can retract into a water sac beneath their eyes. This looks like they're blinking but it's more elaborate than our version of moistening our eyes.

One of the spookiest things a mudskipper can see, other than predators, is another mudskipper. They can be cannibalistic. Hey, we never said they were chillers.

To intimidate each other, protect their territories, and shoo away sexual rivals, they do what most terrestrial animals do. They yell.

The only issue is that they don't have ears and detect vibrations through their body instead. So when they yell at each other, they yell at low frequencies that are hard for us to hear but easier for them to pick up through their bones.

When the tide is high, they hide in burrows for protection. Their little "arms" are great for hopping around in the mud but not great for swimming.

To build these burrows, they use their mouths as wheelbarrows—gulping back mud, carrying it to the surface, and spitting it out. Repeat enough times and you have yourself a burrow—and a dire need of mouthwash.

To protect themselves from predators, they will usually build in twists and turns, which makes it hard for predators to snatch them out of their burrows.

Since the water stuck in their burrows usually becomes oxygen-deficient within a few hours, they bring in air bubbles in their mouth as a backup oxygen tank. So smart.

Their ability to build well-engineered burrows is crucial to their survival as it ensures not only their immediate survival but also their ability to reproduce. During the mating season males fight each other and perform elaborate displays to woo the females. And these fights are epic, floppy, muddy messes.

Males also change colours, becoming brighter, and their throats get shiny and in some species it changes colours. During displays they push themselves up and show off their beautiful throats.

Who doesn't like a good throat? This is called flagging and it's a good indication of health. Healthy males will have brighter throats.

Females will choose their favorite healthy male and follow them to their burrow. They lay the eggs and stick them to the walls of the burrow, and the male fertilizes them. Soon after that, the female leaves, and the male protects the eggs until they hatch.

When they're not in their burrows they're likely hunting. They don't seem like the most menacing of predators but have adapted to catch prey by water-bending.

Atlantic mudskippers carry water in their big mouths. When they're within range of potential prey, they spit some of that water on the prey and then quickly suck it back in. This is done so quickly that the prey ends up being sucked into the mouth along with the water.

In effect they have turned water into their version of a sticky tongue.

This helps them catch a huge array of prey, from worms to flies to crickets to crabs. Imagine being a crustacean and being eaten by a fish out of the water.

This process of gradually getting out of the water is similar to what our latest fish ancestors did before becoming fully terrestrial and tetrapods. Like mudskippers, they likely lived in intertidal environments and gradually became able to spend more time out of the water until that need was eliminated.

When someone asks you how some fish came out of the water, you can show them these guys as examples of fish that gradually became adapted to life on land, just like our ancestors.

Chapter 25
Colugos

Colugos are the strangest almost-primates in the world. We have so much in common with these wide-eyed weirdos, but we're also so different. They glide from tree to tree, they have comb teeth, and they're about the size of a cottontail rabbit. So how did these distant relatives turn out so weird?

Colugos are an evolutionary anomaly. They are the metaphorical mutant lovechild of a tarsier and flying squirrel. Their lifestyle is similar to those of other gliding mammals, who mostly eat fruits and nuts and have evolved to jump from tree to tree. For small animals like these, the air is safer than the ground, which is swarming with carnivores.

Flying squirrels are possibly the most well-known gliding mammals, but this is a successful strategy that has evolved independently several times across many different orders.

But colugos are different.

There is something lemur-like to them, which initially earned them their nickname, "the flying lemurs." That moniker is wrong, but not by much. DNA tests have shown that they're our closest relatives outside of primates.

If you don't see the resemblance between a colugo and, say, a gorilla, it's because our evolutionary paths diverged during the Cretaceous, when dinosaurs still were hunting little mammals. That's a lot of time to change and adapt to new environments.

There are only two remaining colugo species. The Philippine colugo lives in the Southern Philippines, especially in the islands of Mindanao and Bohol. This is the biggest of the two species at just about 1.5 kilograms; it has a mottled coat and a wide face. They're like the pit bulls of the colugos.

And then there's the Sunda colugos, which live in Southeast Asia, from Thailand to Indonesia. They're a little smaller, have solid brown or ginger coats, and a more delicate, pointy face. They're basically colugo greyhounds.

But let's stop beating around the colugo's bushy tail. Colugos have a sort of built-in kite that extends from the wrists to the ankles. It's the maximum amount of coverage that you can have without growing giant wings like bats.

Their squirrel suit is called the patagium, and it's made of leathery skin. On top of that, they have webbed feet to maximize their gliding surface.

To travel between trees, they climb as high as possible and then leap into the wind. With their patagium fully outstretched, they can glide for up to two hundred meters, but jumps of twenty or thirty meters are most common.

As you can imagine from their shape, colugos are not great walkers. Climbing and gliding are their two main methods of transportation, and falling on the ground can be deadly.

Southeast Asia is teeming with predators. While on the tree canopy, Philippine eagles are the greatest threat. But on the ground, several small cat species, as well as foxes, dogs, and dholes can easily catch a colugo.

And so their entire evolutionary history consists of adaptations to help them traverse the forests by climbing and gliding, and doing so at night when no birds of prey are around.

Have you ever walked in a forest at night without a lamp on? It's terrifying. Colugos do that every night while jumping into the void.

Their huge eyes come equipped with giant retinas that give them the night vision and depth perception needed for their leaps. Weirdly, despite being nocturnal, they're thought to have some colour vision.

Primate colour vision evolved after we split off from colugos, but it seems the building blocks were there already, and the ability to see ripe fruits from afar evolved in both orders independently.

Besides predators and gravity, the colugo's biggest problem is rough landings on trees. But, wouldn't you know it, they also have adaptations to protect themselves and their babies from harsh landings.

They have an inbuilt gyroscope that helps them control their speed along the x- and y-axis. When they're in glide mode, they're almost perfectly horizontal so they don't descend as quickly. But when they're about to reach their destination or need to adjust their trajectory to get to the perfect landing spot, they swivel themselves upward.

This slows them down on the x-axis but makes them fall more quickly. So they have to do it at just the right time so that they don't fall to the predator-rich floor.

With all the predators around, it's too dangerous to leave the babies alone in the nest, so moms take them wherever they go.

Colugo babies are born underdeveloped, almost as underdeveloped as marsupial babies. From birth they attach themselves to the mom's belly. The mom uses her tail to build a little pocket for the babies, making a pseudo pouch or baby carrier. And so, moms will carry the babies for months while foraging and will slowly introduce the baby to solid foods.

Colugos have a well-developed digestive system as they need to eat a lot of fiber. When available, most of their meals are fruit salads, with the occasional lichen dessert to get extra minerals.

In times of scarcity, they chew on ants, leaves, bark, and other plant matter.

Their comb-like teeth have the dual purpose of stripping away hard material like bark, lichens, and the tough skin of some fruits, while also being used as a pretty efficient brush to groom themselves to get rid of ticks and other parasites.

Partly because of this diet, colugos are known to have a high parasitic load in their guts. It's so bad that their feces have been reported to move around due to the sheer number of worms in it.

In terms of conservation, both colugo species are considered least concern due to their large range, but there is *some* concern due to the rapid deforestation of the region.

Colugos live in areas that are quickly developing. There are simply fewer trees and those that are still there are more spread apart. In some forest areas, roads are being built, which brings the additional danger of being run over by cars.

There is a current initiative to protect colugo populations by building gliding posts, which are basically utility poles in the middle of the forest or along roads. Colugos can use them as platforms and shorten the distance between leaping locations.

We're still learning about colugos and with the conservation projects in place, we hope we can see these little guys thrive.

Chapter 26
Raccoon Dogs

Raccoon dogs contain multitudes. They're fluffy bandits that strike terror in the hearts of every small creature they meet. To some, they're an invasive menace that threatens wildlife populations across Europe. And to others, they're adorable magical creatures who have charmed the hearts of millions. They have many faces, and they're all masked.

Raccoon dogs are canids and are distantly related to dogs and wolves, though they're more closely related to foxes. They're the only members of the *Nycterectus* genus, but within the genus their taxonomy is a mess.

They're found natively in Japan and continental East Asia. Some scientists believe that the Japanese raccoon dog, also known as

tanuki, is its own species, while others say it's just a subspecies. Others say that only some of the Japanese raccoon dogs are different enough to be considered a separate species.

These hungry hungry creepos have the most varied diet of all canids. They will eat anything, from roots to fish to birds. They have a more well-balanced diet than most of us.

Rodents such as gerbils and voles are commonly taken throughout their range. In swampy areas they eat turtles and poisonous frogs and protect themselves from the toxins by producing extra saliva to dilute the venom. Yep, they drool themselves into being immune to poison.

During the winter, they're able to supplement their diet with carrion and, weirdly, feces.

This varied diet might give them bad breath, but it helps them survive the cold winters. Though they have more survival skills than just having a black hole for a mouth. These ninja-like cuties are masters of stealth.

Raccoon dogs are nighttime specialists. Despite their abundance, few people ever see them, and when they do, it's usually after dusk. This protects the young from diurnal predators such as eagles and humans.

Their eyes are well adapted to low-light conditions, and the iconic black markings around their eyes help them reduce glare. This means that they're less likely to be blinded by bright sources of light. It's a tried-and-true technique that even soldiers and athletes use.

Most importantly, their markings make them look like furry doggy bandits. Their resemblance to trash pandas is a classic case of convergent evolution, and these two omnivorous nocturnal mammals developed similar traits based on their similar habitats and needs.

Like raccoons, who survive the frigid North American winters, raccoon dogs have a dense winter fur that protects them from temperatures as low as -25 degrees Celsius. But unlike their North American lookalikes, raccoon dogs hibernate to survive the lean months. They're the only canids to do so, and, like other hibernating animals, they rely on fat reserves to take them through the winter.

Raccoon dogs will go into hibernation weighing about seven kilograms and come out weighing just half of that. Those who don't get fat enough are unlikely to survive the winter in the colder part of their range, like in Siberia.

So don't be too harsh on them for wanting to eat the world during the warmer months. They need to get as big as a pug by the end of the fall. Yep, that's as big as they get. They're tiny but they look much bigger because of their fur.

Of course, they'll only hibernate when they need to and those in the southern part of their range don't need to hibernate as long.

These wintering adaptations have caught the eye of humans, who see in their fur a marketable product. They have been hunted throughout history to make coats and hats.

Things took a turn in the early twentieth century when Russian trappers brought them to fur farms in the western part of their country to make it easier to get furs without having to import them from thousands of miles away.

This was, what we call in the business, a pretty bad move. As we all know, these fluffy boys are gluttons and can wipe out native species in just a few years. And that's exactly what happened.

Some of those raccoon doggies escaped their fur farms and started breeding in the wild. Since then, they have become invasive in western Russia, the Baltic States, Finland, parts of Sweden, and throughout central and western Europe.

They have been observed as far south as the French-Spanish border. The UK considers it a species likely to become invasive there soon.

Of course, they're only trying to survive and it's not their fault that they were taken from their native range, but they also pose a huge threat to local bird, amphibian, and reptile populations. Because of this, local governments are actively trying to cull them. But these guys are almost ghosts and are nearly impossible to catch without the help of hunting dogs, their natural enemies.

You'd think that since they live in the same areas as bears, tigers, and leopards, they should be easy prey for them. But they're likely too small to be worth the hassle. The bane of their existence is the wolf.

In eastern Russia over half of all raccoon dogs are killed by wolves. Other canids such as foxes and feral dogs often take pups. And for trappers, their success rate increases from 10 percent to 50 percent when employing hunting dogs. It truly is a dog-eat-dog world.

In Japan, tanukis have a better reputation and are the subject of legends.

In local folklore, Japanese raccoon dogs have been said to possess supernatural powers such as shapeshifting and the ability to possess people. These superpowers have been used in media such as Super Mario Bros, where you can get tanuki powers to fly.

The source of their power is thought to be their giant scrotums, which are prominently displayed in tanuki art. Here at *Animalogic* we don't leave any stone unturned, and in the tanuki's stone's case, they were disappointingly average-sized.

But keep on thriving, you magical creatures! We just hope you don't destroy Europe by doing so.

Chapter 27
Porcupines

Porcupines are pig-like creatures that stab their enemies into submission. They have taken over the world by taking on its greatest predators.

There are dozens of species around the world, but they can be easily separated by their home range. Old-world porcupines live in Africa, Asia, and Europe. And new world porcupines are found in the Americas.

Despite their similarities, they're not closely related. New-world porcupines, as well as all other new-world rodents, evolved from rat-like rodents who likely crossed the Atlantic from Africa to South America on rafts.

Regardless of their lineage, they have the same problem on both sides of the pond: giant predators. Lions, tigers, honey badgers, leopards, hyenas, wolves bears, and even sabretooth cats. These pointy pig rats had to get tough or get eaten alive.

The most well-known old-world porcupine is also the largest porcupine in the world. The crested porcupine, which lives throughout Africa and Italy, can be up to twenty-five kilograms and over a meter long, including tail. This makes them the third largest rodent in the world, after capybaras and beavers.

In North America we have the slightly smaller North American porcupines, which are about as long as their African cousins but leaner at about fifteen kilograms. The tropics of Central and South America are home to the tree porcupines. They're smaller but usually weirder.

If you're going on a jungle expedition, make sure you don't let a spiky tree porcupine land on your head and get stuck there. And I'm serious, they fall out of trees a lot.

These spiky guys vary in appearance but they're comfortable in the tree canopy. Predators have a tough time getting up there, but felines have learned to shake them off the trees, so they can turn them over on the ground and bite them in the belly.

There are seventeen new-world species and most of them haven't been properly documented yet, as they live in dense forests, high in the tree canopy, and are famously hard to spot.

They are some of the most alien-looking species in the world, and these are my favorite ones.

The Mexican hairy dwarf porcupine looks like a pig mated with a monkey and their baby joined an '80s glam rock band. They're about the size of a squirrel and live in the tropical rainforests of Mexico and Central America. Jaguarundis, ocelots, and especially margays are their main predators. Their superpower is hanging upside down from their prehensile tail.

Their close cousins, the hairy black-tailed dwarf porcupines are found in northern South America. These guys have long hair that covers their quills. This combo of long bodies and fuzzy hair with spikes underneath gives them a bit of caterpillar vibe, but trust us, these are mammals like you and me.

And finally there's the Brazilian porcupine. This is the most common species in South America and despite their name, they

can be found in every country of the region. Their body is both furry and spiny, and their lighter quills make them look like they have highlights. Their faces are fleshy and pink, which gives them a pig-like appearance.

This superficial resemblance is what gave them their English name. The word *porcupine* is derived from old French and means "spiny pig." Or a squirrel having a bad hair day.

Here in North America, our stabbiest rodent may seem dull in comparison, but it has powerful adaptations to protect itself from predators.

Porcupines have aposematic colouration. They're usually dark brown, but they range in colour from yellow to black with bright white spines. The highlights make their quills more visible to warn predators of their devastating effects. They're serrated and sharp, which means they go into flesh with incredible ease, but their barbs make them difficult and painful to remove. Some predators have been known to carry quills in their mouth and face for years.

The ease with which quills come out of the porcupine's skin made early naturalists believe that they could shoot them, but luckily for all of us who live near them, this turned out to be false.

An adult has about thirty thousand quills that cover most of its body, except for the face and underside. Underneath the skin, they have muscles that can make the quills erect on demand, which is especially when they're trying to signal a predator to back off.

When the quills are standing up, they become easier to detach to impale attackers. At the same time, they emit a smelly liquid odor that sometimes convinces predators that this won't be an easy or delicious meal.

But being covered head to toe in spikes has its downsides, and sometimes porcupines accidentally stab themselves with their own quills. To prevent infections they have developed a coating of antibiotics to keep themselves healthy.

    Imagine being so dangerous that you need to make your own antibiotics!

    Surprisingly, their biggest predator is not the bear or the puma but the deadly fisher, which is basically a tiny tree wolverine. This predator knocks them off trees and tires them out on the ground before turning them over and eating them from the underbelly like a bowl of soup.

    In case you were wondering, when they mate, they put their quills down to prevent accidents. Babies are born with tiny quills that get harder and bigger over time. Aren't they the cuddliest needle balls? Aw.

Chapter 28
SAIGAS

Saigas are antelopes that look like they're straight out of *Star Wars*. Unfortunately, the problems they're facing are far from science fiction.

They're a critically endangered species from the steppes of Central Asia. This is an area that gets incredibly cold in the winter, and to protect themselves from the icy winds they have a feature that makes them look like an alien out of a sci-fi story: their giant, gelatinous-looking nose.

Their nostrils are bloated, significantly enlarged, and pointed downward. Their cavernous nasal passages warm up air entering their nose in the harsh winters of the steppes and cool air entering their nose during hot summers.

Living in large herds in a habitat of semi-desert and plains, there is a lot of dust in the air, and their nose also helps them filter it.

During rutting season, when males are fighting over females, the male's nose gets even bigger! They will shake their heads to attract females, making an extremely satisfying squishy sound as their gelatinous nose shakes side to side. This is their mating ritual. Females choose males with the squishiest, sloppiest, and blubberiest nose.

The second thing you'll notice about saigas is their amazing horns. Only the males have horns, and they can measure up to thirty-five centimeters long and have twenty rings. The older the male, the more rings he has. They use these horns for fighting over females.

Fights for females are common but after the mating season they settle into a peaceful community. Saigas are social animals. They typically form herds of up to forty members, but when migrating they will form massive groups, ten thousand strong. It's an astonishing sight.

Unfortunately, this is a sight that's slowly turning into a mirage. The story of saiga populations is a saga of peaks and valleys. Historically, saigas used to occupy broader territory than they currently do. Prior to the Holocene, they were found from modern-day England, across Europe, Asia, Beringia, Alaska, and possibly even in Canada—but over the years went extinct in most of their range.

More recently, they were almost hunted to extinction in the 1920s, taking their population from the millions to the hundreds. Fortunately, they recovered due to strict protections put in place by the USSR, and, miraculously, thrived despite a thin population bottleneck.

By the 1950s there were two million saigas in the USSR alone.

But all good things must come to an end, and due to their booming population and the dwindling population of another horned species, the rhino, some environmentalists, to curb rhino poaching, encouraged hunters to hunt saiga instead.

This, combined with the fall of the USSR and subsequent loss of saiga protection, led to a free-for-all for the beautiful saiga horn, shrinking their populations. Since the males have the horns, the poachers almost exclusively target them, creating a sex imbalance, resulting in reproductive failures.

Their horns are sought after as trophies and as ingredients for traditional Chinese medicine. Poachers also hunt saigas for their meat, which is considered a delicacy in some parts of Asia.

On top of that, saigas are migratory animals that need to travel vast distances to find better weather and food. Yet, it has become increasingly difficult for saigas to migrate, as barbed-wire border fences stop them from completing their migrations. As a result, many saigas starve to death.

Global warming has allowed new pathogens to enter their environment. Since saigas have gone through two extreme population bottlenecks relatively recently, they aren't well-equipped to fight these new diseases.

Their genetic pool is small, and if there's a disease that will kill one saiga, it's likely to kill thousands.

In 1988, a disease killed over four hundred thousand saigas, over two-thirds of their population at the time. Since then their populations somewhat rebounded, until 2015 when it happened again.

Two hundred thousand saigas died, reducing their population by over half in three weeks.

The most likely cause is a bacterial infection called pasteurellosis, a bacterium found in their noses, and is normally harmless unless it enters the bloodstream, where it becomes lethal.

The leading theory on why this happened is that there were unusually high temperatures and humidity in the days leading up to their deaths, and the same was true for two previous cases of mass death in the region.

This suggests that the rising temperatures across the globe are a key factor in driving these types of deadly bacterial infections.

The most frightening thing about these mass death events is that they have a 100 percent mortality rate. No saiga recovered. When the dust settled, there were only healthy saigas and dead saigas.

Fortunately for saigas, their survival strategy is based on high reproductive rates—with females consistently giving birth to triplets every year. Population booms and crashes might be par for the course, but we're creating a world where the saiga population peaks are low and the valleys are increasingly catastrophic.

Chapter 29
Velvet Worms

The velvet worm has two hot glue guns that shoot ultra-sticky goo out of its head. It has a retractable utility knife built into its mouth opening. And it comes in a range of richly coloured velvet. Is this a crafter's dream? Or a cockroach's worst nightmare?

Onychophora, commonly known as the velvet worm, is a phylum that contains more than two hundred species of super soft, super secretive, super secreters.

Velvet worm skin is covered in a flexible cuticle of chitin, the same tough, protective substance that is the main component in the exoskeletons of arthropods like insects, spiders, and crustaceans. But unlike its arthropod cousins, these creatures are soft and supple, covered in small scales that give it its unmistakable velvety suit.

Velvet worms can be from five micrometers to fifteen centimeters in length and come in a range of fashionable colours. They are most often found in fetching shades of orange, brown, green, black, and blue, with a few cave-dwelling species decked out in all-white. Their velvety skin is prone to drying out, so they live exclusively in areas of high humidity in the southern hemisphere and around the equator.

They are so sensitive to moisture levels in the air that they become noticeably less active during dry periods.

The most "striking" quality of the velvet worm is how it *strikes* both its victims and its predators by squirting them with two sticky streams of self-hardening slime.

Animals squirt for all kinds of reasons. Other than the obvious waste disposal and reproduction, animals will also use the power of the squirt for movement, like squids; as well as for defense, like the horned lizard that shoots blood out of its eyes; and for hunting, like the velvet worm.

This sticky slayer takes the prize for the most unique method of murder.

To locate its prey of crickets, spiders, beetles, termites, cockroaches, and other invertebrates, the predatory velvet worm uses its sensory antenna. Once located, the velvet worm squirts its prey with sticky slime.

The slime is held in large glands in its head segments, like the worm version of Spiderman's web shooters. When ready to attack, the velvet worm shoots goo out of two openings called oral papillae, immobilizing its victims.

Before we get to the terrifying way the velvet worm slices into and liquifies its victims, we need to talk about the utterly unique spray-action of the velvet worm's slime. The velvet worm doesn't just spray its slime straight outward. The high-pressure power of its squirt combined with the elasticity of its oral papillae turn these openings into the equivalent of two out-of-control fire hoses. As a result, the slime oscillates as it sprays upward of thirty centimeters, blanketing its snack in a layer of immobilizing goo.

This fast-action spray may seem to go against the otherwise slow-moving nature of this beast. But because of the syringe-like

structure of the gland and small opening, this slow-poke's slime-squirting muscles don't have to move quickly to result in a powerful spray. When not being used, their rubbery goo guns fold inward like accordions to await their next target.

The slime hardens almost instantly into a glassy texture after it's exposed to air. Once sealed in their glass house of death, the velvet worm moves in for the kill.

Using blade-like jaws that are tucked inside its mouth, the velvet worm slices its way into its prey's exoskeleton and injects it with digestive saliva, which contains mucus and digestive enzymes. Once the insides of its prey are liquified, the velvet worm slurps them out like a milkshake in true horror movie fashion.

Velvet worms also use their slime for self-defense against predators like birds, centipedes, and spiders, although it's not always effective. Hemprichi's coral snakes, which live mostly north of the Amazon River, feed almost exclusively on these squishy squirters.

And squishy they are! They are so flexible, in fact, that they can scrunch themselves into the tiniest crevices, another trait that comes in handy when trying to elude predators or scientists.

Because of their elusive nature, not much is known about their daily lives. But a study of one Australian species, *Euperipatoides rowelli*, showed that some are capable of complex social behavior.

Groups of up to fifteen individuals with complex, female-lead social hierarchies were found to live and hunt together with the

dominant female feeding alone first. Males of the same species will set out to scout out new areas to colonize, like prey-rich decomposing logs, and then secrete a pheromone to attract both males and females to it.

In addition to its super-soaker-like slime throwers, velvet worms are also unique in that their young can be born in one of three ways, depending on the species. Some are oviparous, laying eggs like birds. Some are ovoviviparous, meaning they hatch eggs inside the body like some species of snakes. The most common form of reproduction for this phylum, though, is viviparous, meaning that they birth live young, just like humans!

It seems that's where our similarities with the velvet worm end, unless, of course, you're Peter Parker.

Chapter 30
WOLF EEL

Wolf eels are scary-looking, stretched-out fish that hide and wait for their prey in cracks and crevices, sporting a set of fangs that would make Little Red Riding Hood shudder. They have huge heads and are covered in small scales embedded in the skin, giving them a distinctly "Leatherface" look. But appearances can be deceiving, and the wolf eel is a sweetheart.

Wolf eels inhabit bays and inlets in the temperate North Pacific from the southeastern Bering Sea and eastern Aleutian Islands to Southern California. Although they are called wolf eels, that's a total misnomer. Wolf eels are not *true eels*.

True eels are Anguilliformes, an order of fish encompassing over eight hundred long-bodied species. The wolf eel, a.k.a. *Anarrhichthys*

ocellatus, despite its appearance, belongs to the order Perciformes, which means it's more closely related to grunt sculpins than to true eels.

The wolf eel is monotypic, meaning that it is the only species in its genus *Anarrhichthys*. The other genus, in the Anarhichadidae family, *Anarhichas*, has four species: the Northern, Bering, Spotted, and Atlantic Wolffish, but they're not as long and fun as the wolf eel.

Each of these species has their own special adaptations. The Atlantic wolffish, for example, has no chill. High levels of antifreeze protein in its blood prevent it from getting too cold in the frigid arctic waters.

Wolf eels are the longest and heaviest of these bunch of cousins. They can grow up to two and a half meters or almost eight feet. That's almost a foot taller than Shaquille O'Neal!

Wolf eels swim like a snake slithers on land by propelling themselves forward with s-shaped movements. As juveniles, they stand out in shades of bright orange. As they age, they dull down to more subdued tones of brown and gray covered in a pattern of dark spots as unique to the individual as a fingerprint.

"What big teeth you have!" may have been directed at the wolf in her grandmother's clothing, but Little Red Riding Hood might as well have been talking about the big bad wolf eel. Their teeth are freaky.

They have two kinds of teeth: long and pointed canine-like teeth in the front and heavy molar-like teeth in the back. So although the "eel" part isn't truly accurate, their glinting mouth-knives justify the "wolf" in their name.

Their voracious appetites, forcing them to constantly wolf down prey, also adds a whole other meaning to their moniker.

Wolf eels use their massive jaws of steel to crunch through the hard shells of invertebrates like clams, sand dollars, crustaceans, and even spiny sea urchins! To these echinoderms, these fish truly are the big bad wolf.

If you've ever known the pain of stepping on a sea urchin, imagine swallowing one!

They may look vicious, but wolf eels are mild-tempered with the humans they encounter. There are even cases of them coming out of their dens to interact with divers in the wild.

They also have a tender side, especially when it comes to finding true love. They spend most of their youth on the open ocean, until they meet their forever mate. Then they'll find a cozy den together where they'll both remain for the rest of their lives.

Together these two soulmates will tenderly care for their ten thousand eggs. Once the eggs are fertilized, she uses her body to form them into a ball, which she and her mate will wrap themselves around to protect.

For the four-month incubation period, only one partner will leave to feed at a time, ensuring one stays behind to protect the clutch.

During this time, the mother will constantly shift the eggs to keep them oxygenated. When it's time to hatch, she'll gently squeeze the egg ball to help her little ones emerge.

The lifespan of a wolf eel in the wild isn't entirely understood. In captivity, some live to be over twenty years old. Since the females only reach sexual maturity at around age seven in the wild, it's thought that these fish live long lives. So we say: long live the wolf eel!

Chapter 31
Bush Dog

The bush dog is the weaseliest and weirdest dog you've likely never seen. It might look like a bear/wiener dog mix, but it's a ferocious Amazonian hunter that can take down prey as large as a tapir.

The bush dog is one of the strangest and most elusive dogs in Latin America. It sees everything other wild dogs do and does the opposite. But that rebellious approach to life is what has allowed them to thrive across much of the continent.

They live everywhere from Costa Rica to the northern tip of Argentina. They seem to thrive in tropical rainforests but have also been observed in grasslands, swamps, and pretty much anywhere that gives them enough plant cover and access to water.

OK, a jungle dog that likes water—what's so strange about that? Bush dogs take the wet dog smell to another level.

They're amazing swimmers in part because of their webbed toes and their bodies with small legs make them efficient swimmers. They're the otters of dogs.

Bush dogs can chase prey in water, and, when hunting in packs, they can set traps to force their prey to get into the water, where another bush dog is waiting for them. This strategy is especially effective against rodents like pacas and capybaras, which often jump in the water to escape ocelot and jaguar attacks.

Imagine evading a massive jaguar just to get eaten by a five-kilogram bush dog.

But don't let looks fool you. These canids, which are smaller than beagles, have been observed hunting tapirs, the largest wild animal in the Amazon.

To hunt them, the pack chases the tapir and bites their legs several times until the tapir is felled by ankle injuries and blood loss. It's death by a thousand annoying little cuts. No animal is safe from these dogs.

They, like many other canids, are extremely adaptable and will go for the most abundant prey available.

In the Pantanal region of Brazil, nine-banded armadillos make up over 90 percent of their diet. In the mountain forests of Paraguay, rodents are their favorite meal, and in the Atlantic forest of southern Brazil, where fruit is abundant, they have adapted to eating bananas and papayas almost as much as meat.

Unfortunately we don't know too much about them. They prefer areas that are generally inaccessible to humans, are shy of people, and avoid roads and paths.

They rarely even appear in trap cam pictures. All we know about them is through a few observations and information gathered from native peoples of the region and their behavior in captivity.

They were first described in the 1860s from fossils. At the time they were believed to be extinct, and it was only in the twentieth century that we learned that they were alive.

We know now that they live in groups with a dominant mating pair and a few subordinates. They mate year-round and maintain social cohesion through dog-like behavior such as tail-wagging, squeaks, and signs of submission.

They mark their territories with urine and feces. The smells of these are so pungent that in a huge part of their range they're known as vinegar dogs.

This social behavior helps them hunt in dense forests, where ambush tactics are more effective than straight-line speed. It is a stark contrast with their closest living relative, the maned wolf.

Yep. These two handsome fellas are related. One of the largest canids and one of the shortest ones. The maned wolf is a solitary canid from the South American grasslands. They like to hunt alone, growl at others from a distance, and catch small prey that they can hunt with ease by themselves.

But the more communally oriented bush dogs, which are about a third of the size of a maned wolf, can catch the largest prey there is in their habitats.

So the lone maned wolf got the looks and speed, but the bush dog got the gumption. They have that bush dog spirit in them.

So how did these two cousins end up looking so different? Who was their common ancestor? That, we, unfortunately, don't know for sure.

Animals don't fossilize well in tropical rainforests and those who do are quickly covered by plant matter that makes it almost impossible to find them afterward. But DNA analyses have shown that the bush dog is the more basal dog, meaning that their ancestor resembled them more. It was the maned wolf who had a glow up once it came out of the jungle and into the pampas grasslands.

Unfortunately, deforestation and fragmentation of the rainforest are taking a toll on the bush dog. These little guys are semi-nomadic and need large swaths of land to catch their prey. But as pockets of

their habitat are getting smaller, they're less able to catch the food they need.

Their populations have declined by 25 percent over the past twelve years, and with rainforest deforestation on the rise due to cattle ranching and mining projects, the bush dog is running out of places to hunt and live. Hopefully, as more areas get protected, they can establish stable populations.

So, please support as many rainforest protection initiatives as you can. It will help protect the bush dog and all the amazing Amazonian animals.

Chapter 32
CHEVROTAINS

The chevrotain is a miniature mammal that has the four stomachs of a deer, the fangs of a vampire, the adorable face of a mouse, and one species even swims like a duck. But these squeal-inducing sweeties aren't any of those things. They're ancient creatures that haven't changed much in the past 34 million years.

The chevrotain is the name of the world's tiniest ruminant. Ruminants are even-toed, hoofed animals, usually with four stomachs, like cows, sheep, bison, deer, and antelopes.

Chevrotains have been around for roughly 34 million years, with the highest number of species existing in the Miocene epoch around eleven million years ago. This epoch marks the period when mammals were the newest, hottest creatures on Earth.

Highlights from the Miocene include the emergence of dogs, bears, sabertoothed cats, and whales, to name a few. Dozens of

extinct species of chevrotain have been described in northern Pakistan, Europe, and Africa, but only ten survive today.

Also known as "mouse deer" because of their small stature and rodent-like appearance, these super shy creatures are spread over three genera.

The six species of the *Tragulus* genus and the three of the *Moschiola* genus live in India, Sri Lanka, and Southeast Asia, including Sumatra, Borneo, and Java.

The one exception is the water chevrotain, the chunkiest of them all, who moved far away a couple of million years ago. This is the only species that lives on a completely different continent, making its home in the tropical rainforests of Africa, from Sierra Leone to the Congo.

This lone member of the *Hyemoschus* genus measures around thirteen inches at the shoulder and weighs up to a whopping fifteen kilograms, which is about the weight of a hefty corgi.

Unlike its vegetarian cousins, this species has been known to snack on insects, crabs, and even the occasional dead fish or animal that it comes across.

Chevrotains are famously skittish, which is a great way to elude any potential predator when you're just this small. But the water chevrotain has a slightly wetter and more elaborate escape strategy.

When startled, the water chevrotain will spring into the closest river and swim underwater to elude any suspected predator, which sometimes also includes researchers! It can stay submerged for up to five minutes at a time and propels itself forward by walking along the riverbed. It will come up for air under the cover of river banks and overhanging vegetation to check if the coast is clear.

The water chevrotain is the largest species, but all chevrotains are seriously small. Winning the prize for the world's tiniest ungulate, is *Tragulus kanchil*, the lesser Malayan chevrotain.

The wee-est examples of this diminutive cutie weigh in at just under three pounds. This miniature mouse deer is even the star of a series of fables popular in Indonesia and Malaysia. In these stories, a clever chevrotain named Sang Kancil uses his smarts to outwit those bigger and stronger.

Chevrotains are mostly solitary and elusive animals, which adds to their almost-mythical status. They usually only interact with each other for mating and for the occasional squabble over territory.

Lacking horns or antlers, the males sport tiny fang-like vampiric tusks, which are elongated canine teeth to assist them in their adorable little territorial battles. Not much is known about the habits and behaviors of chevrotains in the wild, however, because they are so darn elusive.

And when I say elusive, I mean elusive! One species, the silver-backed chevrotain, went unspotted for almost thirty years!

It was finally photographed in the wild for the first time in 2017 in southern Vietnam when scientists set up camera traps after receiving some hot tips from locals. These sightings have sparked a push to protect the chevrotain and its habitat.

As you may expect, little is known about the reproductive biology of chevrotains, both in the wild and in captivity, where they are difficult to breed.

To learn more, researchers have even resorted to measuring the hormone levels in the poops of female Java mouse deer to better understand their reproductive physiology. That's what I call dedication to this adorable ungulate!

Chapter 33
Red-Lipped Batfish

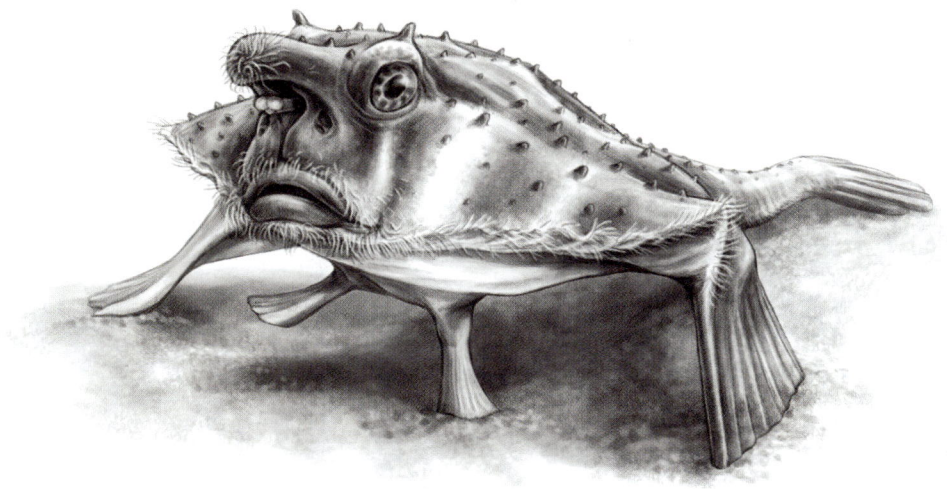

The red-lipped batfish is one of the weirdest fish in the world. There's no doubt about it. They have weirdly human red lips, fins for legs, a beard, and bioluminescent parts. This Galapagos local looks like a hoax made with AI, but it's real, it's fierce, and it's thriving.

When you look at a red-lipped batfish, the immediate question is usually, why? What evolutionary forces could have possibly led to a fish looking like this?

There are still a lot of unresolved mysteries, but let's go one ridiculous feature at a time, starting with their supple little lips.

Yes, they look like someone applied a beauty filter to a clam, but their purpose is surprisingly relatable. They're just trying to look cute. Or at least that's the current leading theory.

Red-lipped batfish have a dual strategy of being well camouflaged if you look at them from above and being recognizable when face to face. Their predators usually swim over them, but they encounter other batfish at eye level.

Their beautiful lips are for them to recognize each other when it's time to mate. Love is in the air, but it's also underwater.

Something to consider is that red light doesn't travel well through water. The deeper you go, the bluer everything looks. It's not because the water is blue but simply because red light is the first one to disappear underwater.

So having aggressively red lips is a way to stand out in a literal ocean of blue.

Additionally, we're still not sure how good colour vision is in batfish. They might not perceive red the same as we do. So at their maximum depth, around seventy-five meters, they might look to each other like mostly black and white, like goth-lipped batfish.

All around their bodacious lips they have little beard-like projections that make them look like they haven't shaved for a couple of days. The purpose of these wispy beards is currently unknown.

There's a lot more to these cute fish than their cherry lips. Everything about them is bat-fish crazy.

On top of their head they have a sort of horn, which, as you might expect by now, we have no idea what it's for, but it's common among all their batfish cousins. Many of them have large, pointy, front-facing horns.

A clue about their origin can be found in their other relatives. They're part of the anglerfish order, which have lots of species with a horn, usually called an illicium.

At the tip of the illicium there's a bioluminescent lure called an esca. In different species the esca might look like a little worm or other invertebrate to attract small fish, which are then ambushed and swallowed whole by the anglerfish. A classic case of aggressive mimicry.

Batfishes also have lures, but they don't come out from where you'd expect.

While most anglerfish have their lure at the tip of their fishing rod, red-lipped batfish and its siblings have it come from an orifice at the base of the horn. It almost makes it look like it's snot, but it's not.

The lure collects bioluminescent bacteria from the ocean, which is key for attracting prey at the deepest parts of their range.

Of course getting down there is a whole other thing. Batfish are as good at swimming as bats are at walking. Their fins have instead adapted to walking pretty much like baby kangaroos walk before they learn to hop: awkwardly and with limbs that seem too big for their body size.

If they have to swim, they'll tuck their fin legs under their body and propel themselves with their pointy tails.

Some closely related bad swimmers, like the frogfish, use jet propulsion by gulping water and then forcing it out of their gills.

They look silly doing it, but it helps for a little burst of speed for otherwise slow species, especially when they're young and most vulnerable.

Nobody knows for sure if batfish can do this. There are no reports of this behavior, but when they swim you can see two openings at the back of their fins open similarly to animals with jet propulsion.

It's possible that they had jet propulsion at some point in their evolutionary history, but it might have become useless since they don't seem to have many predators.

There are no reports of predation on these guys. They do, after all, look like they would taste funny.

But they might have several predators and we just haven't seen them eating red-lipped batfish. They live in the waters of the Galapagos islands, home to predators like Galapagos sharks, white-tip reef sharks, and, of course, Galapagos penguins.

There might be an epic Batfish versus The Penguin battle happening right now, and we don't have a way to find out.

Yet another riddle about these adorable freaks. Please, science, catch up; we need to know what's going on with the red-lipped batfish.

But we have to admit there are a few reasons why it's so hard to study them. They are sometimes seen in waters as shallow as three meters, but most of their range is below where most divers can go.

Even if you were to swim near them, unless you shine a bright light on them, it's most likely that you'd miss them due to their colourization and texture. They look like a rock or a coral from above.

They're also known to have a large parasitic load so they might not live too long in the wild. When they're caught to be put in an aquarium, they have to go through a tough deworming process, but aquarists have figured out how to keep them for up to twelve years. Maybe we'll get some insights from them.

You'd think that a fish as magnificent as this would have hordes of scientists diving in Galapagos to learn more about them, but they're surprisingly understudied. The red-lip was first described in 1985, which is a while ago but not nearly as much as some of its cousins, like the polka dot batfish, which has been known since 1818.

The red-lipped batfish is an anomaly in a land of weirdos. Even its scientific name, *Ogcocephalus darwini*, reminds us of the amazing power of evolution to create the strangest things imaginable. But we need to learn more about it.

If you're a marine biologist, consider researching this fish so we can update this book with some of these riddles solved.

Chapter 34
South American River Dolphins

The South American River Dolphin is a murky water hunter with a sixth sense for finding fresh meat. Their pink skin makes them stand out in the darkness of the Amazon rainforest. Some might say it's the prettiest cetacean on Earth, and if you ask the locals they'll tell you it might steal your heart and take it to the depths of the Amazon River.

When you think of Amazonian apex predators you probably think of harpy eagles, jaguars, and caimans. But in the rivers and flooded jungles lives a deadly predator with the face of an angel.

Maybe angel-faced is pushing it but Amazonian river dolphins are cute killers, though maybe not as charismatic as their cousins, the bottlenose dolphins. They're one of several river dolphin species in South America.

There's some taxonomic controversy, but the species usually recognized are the Bolivian river dolphin, the Araguaian river dolphin of Brazil, the Amazon river dolphin, and the Orinoco river dolphin. Some scientists claim they're all subspecies of the same species, so for simplicity's sake, we'll call them all by their common name: botos.

Botos evolved from marine dolphins. Nobody knows for sure when they got to South America. They could have entered the continent from the Atlantic through the Amazon delta, but it's possible that they entered it from the Pacific side before the formation of the Andes.

These river dolphins are thousands of kilometers away from their closest seafaring relative, the La Plata dolphin, the only river dolphin known to live in saltwater estuaries, as well as the coast of the South Atlantic.

Though the boto's biology differs from marine dolphins in fundamental ways. Marine dolphins, such as the common dolphins, or the bottlenose, are built for speed. They have to travel vast distances in search of food and will catch fish in the open water. Their double-slitted eyes work equally well in and out of the water. And they're able to dive up to forty meters in search of fish.

Botos, on the other hand, are built for agility. The levels of the rivers they live in can fluctuate up to twelve meters depending on the season. When the levels are high, the river floods the jungle,

and fish head there as it's safer than in the open river and offers more feeding opportunities.

Botos need to be able to follow their prey into those flooded environments full of obstacles. That's why being smaller and more pliable is a must when navigating and hunting in the flooded jungle.

While bottlenose dolphins are about 4 meters long and weigh up to 300 kilograms, botos are just over half the weight of a bottleneck and are just about 2.5 meters long. Boto females are even smaller, which is unique among river dolphins. In Asian species females tend to be larger than males.

Marine dolphins are built like arrows. Their neck vertebrae are fused to keep them straight when swimming at high speeds.

Boto's vertebrae are not fused. This allows them to turn their head 90 degrees.

Because of their fused necks, when they surface for air, bottlenoses have to make a bigger jump. Botos are more flexible and only have to come out slightly to expose their blowholes.

That doesn't mean they can't jump though. They have been documented jumping over three meters out of the water.

But while a marine cetacean like a Dall's porpoise can swim at seventy kilometers an hour, and a bottlenose can reach speeds of thirty-five kilometers an hour, a boto can only swim at twenty kilometers an hour, though normally they only swim at a leisurely three kilometers an hour. They're the slow walkers of the dolphin family.

We've been kinda burying the lead here, but yes, botos are adorably pink. But unlike flamingos and other pink birds who get their colouration from their food, botos get them from scraping their body on rocks and plants.

So yep, they're basically covered in scars. But it's cool; boto chicks dig scars.

In general, older males will be pinker because in addition to having to swim in rough areas, they'll fight each other for access to females.

Botos are less gregarious than marine dolphins usually hanging out in duos or trios. Though, because of the nature of their habitat, they're found in higher densities than other dolphins in their ecosystems.

They have a lot of neighbors but not a lot of friends.

Some exceptionally large groups of over thirty dolphins have been documented, but they're extremely rare. During the rainy season the females and the young spend most of their time in the flooded forest, while males stay in the river.

That doesn't mean that males get less of a meal. South American tropical rainforests are packed with all sorts of yummy food.

And if you're starting to think they are not as brutal as their saltwater relatives, you better reconsider. One of the boto's favorite meals is piranhas.

During the dry season, when all the fish are concentrated in a relatively small area, botos can be picky with their food, but during the flooding season, they catch whatever they can.

They've been observed cracking open freshwater crabs and turtles. These adorable predators eat about 5 percent of their body weight every day. And the biggest key to their hunting success is their echolocation.

Botos have a huge echolocation organ on their head, officially and hilariously called a melon, which helps them find their way in the dark and murky waters of the rainforest. But since the jungle is full of trees and rocks and sandbanks, the echo from a single click might be too confusing.

So they produce about eighty clicks per second to give them constantly updating spatial mapping of their surroundings.

Their clicks aren't nearly as loud as those of dolphins in marine environments, whose echoes have to travel longer distances in the open ocean. But botos don't need them to travel as far since their hunting grounds are smaller.

Botos are deeply entrenched in several Amazonian cultures' folklore. They're often portrayed as seductive shapeshifters who can take on the shape of a handsome man who attends parties and lures beautiful women to the river.

Unfortunately their charm doesn't protect them from fishermen, who often accidentally catch them and other river cetaceans like tucuxis in their nets, where the botos suffocate to death. More recently, some fishermen have come to use river dolphin meat as bait. Others deliberately kill them because they damage fishing equipment. This has led to a rapid decline in their populations.

The Amazonian river dolphin is an endangered species and local governments have banned the killing of dolphins and put a moratorium on fishing species caught with boto meat, such as the piracatinga, a scavenger catfish.

Hopefully, as more people become aware of their plight they'll become better protected, and we might see them again in human form 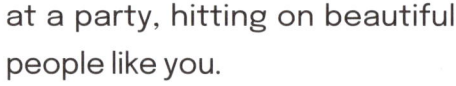 at a party, hitting on beautiful people like you.

Chapter 35
CAPYBARA

The capybara is a rodent that swims like a hippo, with its ears, eyes, and nostrils remaining above water. It chews like a camel, from side to side rather than up and down. It has been mistaken for a pig, barks like a dog, and is equally at home on land and in the water. This is one of the strangest rodents in the world.

When you think of rodents you probably imagine rats, squirrels, and other tiny creatures. Well, make room for the king of rats. The capybara is the largest rodent in the world, with an average adult weighing over fifty kilograms.

That's sixty times more massive than their closest living relatives, the rock cavy!

The capybara is the last remnant of a long line of gigantic grass-eating rodents that evolved in South America over millions of years ago. When explorers first observed capybaras in the wild, they were mistaken for relatives of pigs—today we know they are more closely related to guinea pigs than to Babe, the gallant pig.

Their name originates from the Indigenous South American Tupi language, which, in the sixteenth century was the most widespread language in the continent. The word *capybara* comes from the Tupi word "kapii'gwara," meaning "grass eater."

Capybaras—sometimes shortened to capys—can be found in Central and South America, wherever standing water is readily available.

Water is a vital resource for capybaras. In fact, these semi-aquatic creatures have several adaptations to life in bodies of water. They have small eyes, noses, and hairless ears located high on their heads, which allow them to keep only part of their faces exposed when their bodies are submerged.

They even have special flaps on their ears to keep water out.

Their reddish to dark brown fur is long and brittle, perfect for drying out quickly on land. And they're great swimmers, due in part to their slightly webbed feet.

Capybaras can stay underwater for an impressive four to five minutes at a time when hiding from predators, which are usually felines such as jaguars, pumas, and ocelots.

They're so comfortable in the water that they can even mate and sleep while partially submerged! So, as you can imagine, a year-round standing water source is essential for the capybara's survival.

Capys are herbivores and use their long sharp teeth to eat a variety of water plants and grasses. Like all rodents they have ever-growing front teeth. It's a necessary adaptation since they wear their teeth down daily.

An adult capybara can eat over four kilograms of grass every day. But they're not picky and during the dry season when grasses aren't readily available, they eat grains, melons, and squashes. But their diet doesn't end there.

Capybaras have another more unusual food source that they don't have to go far to find. Capybaras engage in cecotrophy, a fancy word for eating your own poop.

Capybaras are hindgut fermenters. Grasses go through their stomach and then get fermented in their intestine. This helps break down the fibers and creates a more nutritious meal. Unfortunately, since the stomach is before the intestines in the digestive tract, they have to poop the fermented food out and then eat it again.

Capybaras are highly social animals who exhibit complex social behaviors and live according to a strict hierarchy. A herd of capybara ranges in size from five to a crowded hundred giant rodents, with bigger groups tending to form in the dry season.

Capybaras are extremely territorial when it comes to their social groups. They use their scent glands to mark their territory with chemicals. The glands are located by their nostrils, which makes it easier to smear secretion on vegetation.

They may also mark vegetation by dragging their anal gland across it or by urination. Hey! Whatever it takes to mark your territory, especially when prime real estate can give you access to the best year-round food!

Within a social group, females tend to reproduce around the same time, with most females giving birth within a period of two weeks at the end of wet season. This allows their young to benefit from communal nursing. You know what they say—it takes a village! And that's especially true of capybaras.

Young capybaras emit a characteristic whining or whistling frequently throughout the day, to maintain contact amongst themselves and their mothers. During the first year of life, the young are extremely vulnerable to predators, so their ability to whistle throughout the day is a matter of life or death!

Capybara communication is composed of several different sounds. In addition to the whistles associated with infants, there are also barks associated with potential predators, other barks that assert dominance, and chuckles between individuals traveling together.

These sounds seem to be group-specific. Social groups have distinct vocalizations that are not recognized or understood by other groups of capybaras!

When they're not avoiding predators, capybaras have a calm and laid-back temperament. And this friendliness even extends to other species.

On any given day, you may find a capybara with a bird companion or two. This is because there are several species, with whom they have a symbiotic relationship. The birds will happily eat parasites on the capybara's fur. So that's what they mean when they say a feather on your cap!

Capybaras are hunted by humans for their meat and hide, and their habitat has decreased due to human activity, but their populations are currently stable across much of their range. We love a cappy ending!

Chapter 36
Stargazers

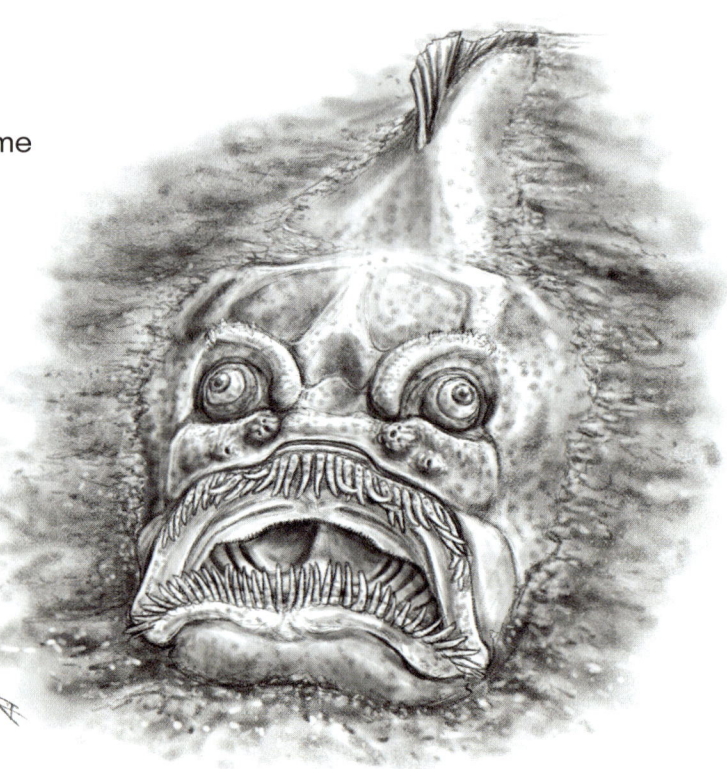

When you hear the name stargazers, you probably imagine a cute, romantic, wistful-looking fish. But you'd be wrong. The stargazer is an electric, venomous, monster of the sea, and a possible new addition to our nightmares.

Stargazers are fish of two families, electric stargazers and sand stargazers. We're going to focus on the electric stargazers.

Stargazers look like two different creatures: one, an oddly shaped fish when swimming around, and the other, a vaguely human-monster hybrid when they're buried in the sand.

It's this second form that they get their romantic name from. Stargazers are ambush hunters, adept at burying themselves in sand and waiting for prey to swim by. When it does, they shoot out from hiding, creating a vacuum with their oral cavity that sucks prey into their oversized mouths.

Their bites are breathtakingly fast, capturing prey within 150 milliseconds.

There are over twenty different species of stargazers, ranging in size from fifteen centimeters to just under a meter long, and they can be found all over the world in relatively shallow water, usually between five and one hundred and fifty meters deep.

Being ambush hunters, stargazers are not picky eaters but usually find themselves eating unsuspecting small fish, crustaceans, and cephalopods.

To dig themselves into the ocean floor, they have large, shovel-like fins, perfect for burrowing in and waiting for prey.

In case you were thinking these amazing little monsters weren't frightening enough, they are both venomous and electric. Their venom is located in two sharp, long, bony spines on their back that can fold down. Stargazers use their venom to deter predators and kill prey.

They sting humans fairly often, but the venom isn't usually lethal. However, there have been several reported fatalities from the Mediterranean species *Uranoscopus scaber*.

Stargazer venom is a mystery. Scientists haven't been able to determine what their venom is or how it works. When they tried to remove the venom from their glands, they couldn't confirm any toxicity in the substance—scientists believe this is because their venom is highly unstable.

As we mentioned before, stargazers are not only venomous but capable of creating electric shocks! Many species of stargazer come equipped with electroplaxes, which are stacks of polarized, flattened muscle cells that function somewhat like a capacitor. They're capable of producing a fifty-volt shock—potentially enough to scare off predators, but not quite enough to stun prey, as some researchers had previously thought, though its specific function is still unconfirmed.

This electric organ is located behind their eyes and, when triggered, creates a current that flows throughout the body of the fish. This whole process is incredibly fast and is over in milliseconds. To make another zap, they'll need to charge their batteries by snacking on prey.

While they usually create short bursts of electric energy, occasionally, during spawning, stargazers will create a longer burst of electricity lasting several seconds to help them find mates.

Some species of stargazers come equipped with lures to help them snag prey. These resemble worms that are attached to a fishing-rod-like appendage on their lower lip.

If you look closely at their mouths, you'll see that they look like zippers. In fact, the mouth of the stargazer is interlocked with tiny bristles that prevent sand from falling into their mouths when they're buried. A system that works about as well as it can but still lets some sand in when they open their mouths to grab dinner.

But stargazers have a second lure as well! This one is their specialized gills. These will discharge sea water next to their pectoral fin, which causes the sand to swirl around as if a small fish were present. When a larger fish comes to check it out, the stargazer opens its mouth and snaps it up.

They will also use their eyes to lure in prey. Once a small fish is almost in range, the star gazer will rotate one of their contralateral eyes to give the impression that a small burrowing creature is there—this will draw in a curious fish, before, you know, the super quick bite takes place.

As if these little monsters didn't have enough going for them, some species, like the black sea stargazer or *Uranoscopus scaber*, come equipped with the ability to create acoustic pulses. They can emit a low-frequency acoustic discharge between five and ten hertz—just below the human hearing threshold—which researchers believe they use to stun prey and appear stunning to their potential mates.

Funny how those two abilities often coincide, isn't it?

Chapter 37
Garter Snakes

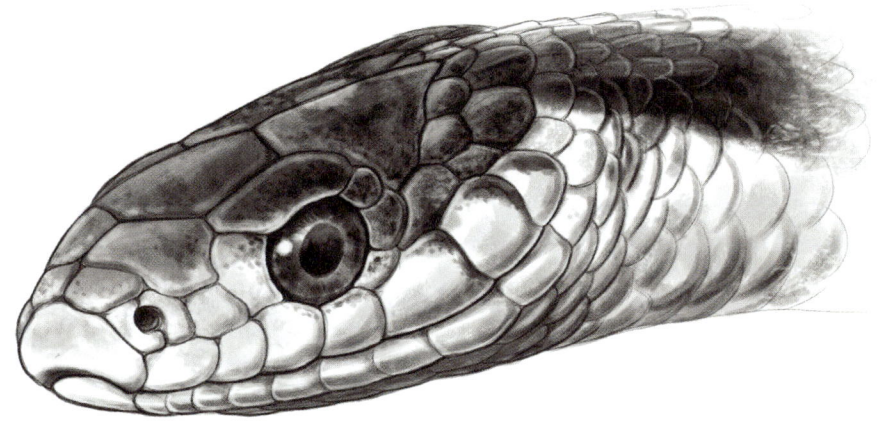

Red-sided garter snakes live in one of the largest snake gatherings in the world: the Narcisse snake dens. They can look like a scary place, but thousands of people flock to this place to see fifty thousand snakes mate in a series of mating balls.

The Narcisse snake dens in Manitoba, Canada, and is such an iconic place that it was nominated to be one of Canada's seven natural wonders. It didn't win because people seem to prefer the Rocky Mountains to mountains made of snakes.

For some people, this is the stuff of nightmares, but to us, it's a dream come true.

This is the largest agglomeration of red-sided garter snakes in the world. There are snakes as far as the eye can see!

These are a subspecies of the incredibly widespread garter snake *Thamnophis sirtalis*. There are subspecies all over North America, from the Northwestern territories of Canada to the Chihuahuan Desert, Mexico.

They live in a variety of environments. From the eastern garter snake who roams the forests of the Atlantic Coast to the Puget Sound garter snake who makes its way through the rainforests of British Columbia to the New Mexico garter who weathers the arid conditions of the deserts of the American Southwest.

They all look different as they have adapted to match all their environments better.

The red-sided garter snakes are more colourful up close than you might think.

Even though they're called red-sided, the Narcisse population is mostly dark brown with yellow stripes alongside their body. They're about 150 grams and are on average about a meter long, though older individuals can be much longer than that.

Around Mother's Day, they come out of a hibernation-like stupor called a brumation.

The location is unexpected. Manitoba, maybe most well-known as one of the best places to see polar bears, doesn't come across as a snake haven. But the secret to its hospitality is its rocks.

The Narcisse area has massive deposits of water-worn limestone bedrock. These rocks are known to crack and make deep tunnels that the snakes can use to hide away from the winter cold.

Manitoba winters are brutal, and the soil freezes a few meters below ground level. Frozen soil is lethal to snakes, but the limestone cracks allow them to go deeper into warmer areas.

Their depth is only limited to the wet soil farther below called the water table, which is the upper limit of natural deposits of water.

So their sweet spot is the pockets of air between the ice and the water. Claustrophobic if you ask me, but they seem to like it.

Once they get over their winter slumber, it's springtime. The frogs are croaking, flowers are blooming, and snakes come out to look for a mate.

Unfortunately this can be a problem for them as there is a large sex imbalance. There can be between ten and a hundred males for every single female so the competition is fierce.

Older and larger females are more fertile and attract the largest and most powerful males. While trying to mate, they'll wrap around her and lift her tail with their own tails—yeah, snakes have tails—and try to copulate.

As nice as it is to have your choice of male mate, this can be a huge hassle for females, who at this point are more interested in food than in the boys trying to slither into their DMs.

Things are even tougher for younger females. Sometimes they essentially get kidnapped and can't get away until they mate with the males. Females under the age of three are usually infertile but they get harassed by boys. This limits their chances of survival as it delays their return to their feeding grounds.

Some males have skin oils with female pheromones, and they too get chased by other males, which they would lead astray and then return to the females with less competition. These males with female pheromones are thought to have more reproductive success than other males, and for decades, this was considered a great example of sexual mimicry.

But more recent studies have pondered whether the pheromones were there all along, and most males adapted to not having them to avoid being chased by other males.

It's kind of a chicken-and-the-egg question.

In any case, females do everything they can to evade all these guys and get to their pond as quickly as possible to get some delicious snacks, after all, at this point they haven't eaten in months.

Speaking of food, garter snakes hunt a huge variety of prey. Living in such disparate locations, the different subspecies specialize in whatever is most available in their habitat.

Garter snakes from the West Coast have even adapted to eat poisonous rough-skinned newts, one of the most poisonous amphibians in the world. These amphibians produce a neurotoxin called tetrodotoxin, the same poison found in pufferfish. In some populations they have enough of it to kill ten to twenty humans.

But garter snakes are built differently and they can catch them, though they usually get lethargic and cold after digesting their prey. These snakes are the only animal known to eat rough-skinned newts and live to taste the tail. And even more so, some of the tetrodotoxin stays in the body of the snake making it also poisonous to predators.

There are a lot of predators around the Narcisse snake dens, from crows to owls to large frogs. There is some safety in numbers, but the sheer number of easy-to-catch snakes attracts a few predators. And who can blame

them? If I knew my favorite food would magically pop up from a hole in the ground, I'd be waiting too.

These snakes, though relatively docile, are not completely defenseless. When threatened they can snap, take a threatening pose, or try to make a speedy getaway. The venom is not as toxic as other snakes in their region such as rattlesnakes, but they can still cause a lot of pain and irritation.

Unfortunately, they can't stay active for too long, and some, especially younger snakes, get exhausted and become easy pickings for their predators.

Given all their issues it seems like they should have been eaten to extinction by now, but luckily they're good at reproducing. One mature snake can lay up to forty eggs, though younger females lay fewer eggs, and first-time moms only lay one to five eggs.

But since there are relatively few females, each of them is crucial for the survival of the species. Some populations have disappeared or become just a tiny fraction of what they were due to the extirpation of females.

Pest control affects them because even if they don't eat the poison, sometimes they catch prey that has consumed it and become poisoned themselves.

Car accidents unfortunately happen and in 1999 this population crashed due to extremely bad weather and nearly ten thousand snakes being run over every year.

The numbers got so low that migration tunnels were built under the roads and though accidents are a reality of life, fewer than a thousand snakes get killed that way every year.

Habitat destruction due to limestone mining has completely collapsed some of their denning sites. Luckily some areas, like Narcisse, are fully protected and hopefully will continue to be a haven for the beautiful red-sided garter snake.

Chapter 38

Japanese Macaques

Japanese macaques live high in the mountains of Japan and have become better adapted to the cold than any other primate, excluding humans. But like us, they have found novel ways to deal with the frigid winters. They go to the spa.

These monkeys are found on three of the four main Japanese islands: Honshu, Shikoku, and Kyushu. They live in a variety of different habitats, including evergreen and deciduous forests, sub-tropical lowlands, and subalpine regions up to 1,500 meters high.

The monkeys are more comfortable in the warm weather. But they've managed to adapt well to regions with freezing cold, snowy winters. In fact, other than humans, they're the only primates that can survive that far north. Because of this they're also known as "snow monkeys."

Japanese macaques are medium-sized monkeys, with the males slightly larger than the females. Macaques that live in colder climates tend to be heavier than the southern ones. The added weight helps them deal with the cold.

Another feature that helps them survive the freezing temperatures is their long, lush brownish or gray coats, which grow extra-thick in the winters for insulation. Their faces are naked and a pinkish red, with long beards, giving them a human-like appearance. Their red rump matches their face. Cute!

The macaques that live in colder climates have to deal with temperatures that can get down to -15 degrees Celsius. Sure, they've got their extra-thick winter coats, and they manage to survive the nights by huddling together in trees. But there's gotta be another way to escape the freezing cold. A dip in a hot spring.

The story goes that in the 1960s, a young snow monkey living in the Nagano mountains took an accidental bath in a local hostel's hot spring, heated up by a nearby volcano.

The other monkeys gradually started doing the same thing, possibly inspired by watching the humans do it. Soon the humans got a little annoyed that the macaques were interrupting their spa day. After all, sharing bathwater with monkeys isn't the most hygienic practice. So the locals kindly built the macaques their own private hot springs.

Decades later macaque troops bathe in their personal pools every single day. They get warm, groom, socialize, bond, and relax. Their special hot tub time has also become a major tourist attraction.

The monkeys don't seem to mind the curious humans. They're more concerned about soaking away the stresses of their day.

Macaques are incredibly intelligent, social creatures. They live in troops that can range anywhere from a few monkeys to several hundred.

A dominant male leads troupes. Females always stay in the same group they're born into, but the males have to leave before sexual maturity. They'll find mates in other troupes. This helps ensure genetic diversity. So smart!

The group's alpha male has a lot of responsibilities. He has to sire the young, protect his babies from predators and other macaques, decide where his troop goes, and remind lesser monkeys who's the boss!

The females spend a lot of time raising the young monkeys and grooming, which includes getting rid of tangles, and parasites.

Snow monkey troops are always on the move. They're omnivores, and their favorite foods are smaller animals and plants, mainly fruits, berries, seeds, flowers, and young leaves. They also dine on insects, crabs, and bird eggs during the winter.

Their opposable thumbs help them skillfully rummage through thick winter snow to find food. If a winter snowfall is heavy, the monkeys rely on eating bark and buds. And if the pickings are slim they'll try scavenging fungi.

Social rank is important in a Japanese macaque's world. There is a strict chain of command. A male's rank is usually determined by his age. Other monkeys inherit their social standing through their mother's rank.

The odd time an extremely clever or aggressive monkey can move up the social ladder and take its family with it.

Japanese macaques can have several partners during mating season, which lasts four or five months between September and

April. Females are picky, and they choose their mates by… you guessed it! Rank!

Sometimes monkeys fight over who gets to mate with who. Usually the winner of a fight comes down to which macaque can scream the loudest.

But during mating season, things can get physical! Sometimes they'll even bite! And check out those strong, sharp chompers! I wouldn't wanna mess with a macaque!

After mating, the female macaque gestates for about six months. Babies are usually born in the spring and summer. Just one. The babies are dependent on their mothers and will cling to them for the first two years of their lives.

As they grow, the monkeys will learn socializing and macaque hierarchy by mingling in the hot springs, play and play-fighting in the snow, and even making snowballs! They'll also play with stones and fight and swing in the trees. In the winter they sleep in the deciduous trees to prevent accumulated snow from falling on top of them.

They sound like a handful. No wonder the moms need to unwind at the spa!

Once they're weaned, the male monkeys will leave their troops, and spend the rest of their lives traveling between and mating between other troops.

Sounds stressful. I wonder how the Japanese macaque can find a way to relax...

Chapter 39
Siberian Musk Deer

Siberian musk deer have the face of a kangaroo, the fangs of a vampire, and a shy soul with an irresistible musk desired the world over.

They can be found in the mountains and grasslands of Northeast Asia, but they're most commonly found in the snowy mountain forests of Siberia. Hence their name.

Despite being called deer, they have more in common with animals in the Ovidae family than the "true deer" in the family Cervidae. They are in their own family, and are closer to antelopes, cows, sheep, and goats than to reindeer, elk, red deer, and moose.

For one thing, male Siberian musk deer don't have antlers like their cervid friends. Instead they have a pair of tusks that look like fangs. They can reach about ten centimeters long and never stop growing their whole lives. Older males have the largest teeth.

Cervids have preorbital glands near their eyes, which they use to mark their scent, communicate with other animals, and spray pheromones. But the musk deer's scent glands aren't on their faces. They're all the way around back...

Yep! Right there! In a little golf ball-sized sack in front of their genitals.

This musk gland is what makes them musk deer. The males spray their musk to mark their territory and attract females for mating. And the odor is so, so strong.

That powerful musk is a pro and a con for the male Siberian musk deer. Pro: the pheromones help them attract females in mating season. The con? They're being poached for it. A lot.

For the last five thousand years, people have been obsessed with capturing and selling their musk glands so they can be used in perfume, medicine, and luxury items. In the early '70s, musk glands were so valuable in Nepal that they were worth more than gold.

Besides poaching, musk deer have to worry about finding food in the cold vastness of their range. They're ruminants, meaning they eat relatively calorie-poor food that gets fermented in their digestive tract to extract all the available nutrients.

Siberian musk deer are herbivores despite their scary-looking fangs. They love eating pine needles, leaves, bark, maple, honeysuckle, shoots, but mostly lichen.

They forage for it at night, sometimes traveling kilometers at a time on well-worn tracks they create and use over and over. In the cold winters, when food is scarce, the Siberian musk deer can survive on lichens that grow on evergreen trees. They make up to 99 percent of their winter diet.

The musk deer find lichen by climbing bent tree trunks that can take them up to four meters in the air.

Don't worry, they're not scared of heights. They're frequently found on steep, mountainous slopes, just like their goat cousins.

Siberian musk deer are shy and cautious animals, who are mostly active at dusk and nighttime. They're typically found by themselves or in small groups of two or three. And usually those groups are a momma musk deer with their babies.

The deer's small body helps it run fast and hide from predators in tiny openings in the rocky terrain. They have to watch out for threats like lynx, wolverines, and the yellow-throated marten.

When they notice danger, they raise their tails to helpfully alert the other members of the musk deer community.

Musk deer are migratory animals. In the winter they live on steep slopes covered with coniferous trees. While they can move easily on top of snow because of their light weight, navigating deep, loose snow can be difficult and dangerous. When this kind of snow blocks their familiar paths for food, they must create new accessible winter paths.

In the summer they move down to grassy meadows along the river valleys of their mountain homes. During the spring and fall Siberian

musk deer use communal toilets, which obviously produce a strong odor. The deer use the smell of their feces to communicate with one another.

Not much is known about how Siberian musk deer mate. Mating season is in November and December. That's when young male deer develop their tusks, which threaten rival males and impress members of the opposite sex.

And don't forget about their musk glands, which secrete powerful, mate-attracting pheromones.

After mating, it takes about six months of gestation before one or two fawns are born in late spring. Females give birth in special areas, under dense shrubs, low branches of fir, or around fallen trees.

The babies live with their mothers until they're two, although they reach sexual maturity around sixteen months old.

Because of illegal poaching and deforestation, musk deer populations are declining. The species is considered vulnerable, and they're headed toward becoming endangered.

So please, poachers, stick to your own natural musk! Let the Siberian musk deer eat their lichen, grow their tusks, and hang out on mountains!

Chapter 40

PANGOLINS

T he pangolin is a prehistoric eater of ants, covered head to toe in scales, and one of the most heavily poached animals in the world. They look like the offspring of an anteater and a pinecone.

Until recently they were thought to be related to armadillos, for obvious reasons, but DNA tests have shown they're more closely related to lions, walruses, and pandas than to their armored lookalikes.

There are eight extant species of pangolins, four in Asia and four in Africa. They vary in size greatly. The smallest of them is the long-tailed pangolin at roughly thirty centimeters long, excluding the tail, and the largest is the aptly named "giant pangolin" at 1.8 meters long, excluding the tail.

They are covered head to toe in beautiful, defensive scales, which look a lot like scale armor. In fact—King George III was presented with a suit of armor made of pangolin scales in 1820.

Pangolin scales are similar to reptile scales and are made out of keratin–the same material that makes up our fingernails. In fact, pangolins the only known mammal to have scales at all.

Their scales, which overlap with each other, are fantastic for warding off ant and termite bites and for fending off predators. When attacked by carnivores like lions or hyenas, the pangolin curls up into a ball, tucking their head under their armored tail, making itself virtually impenetrable.

Not only do their scales make it near impossible for them to be chewed on by lions, but the edges of the scales are sharp–making them even less appealing as an afternoon snack.

But, if a pangolin is caught before it has a chance to roll up, it will defend itself by thrashing its long, muscular tail back and forth, cutting its attacker with its sharp scales.

The diet of the pangolin consists almost exclusively of ants and termites, and like anteaters they have a long and sticky tongue to grab their meal.

In some species their tongue can be longer than their bodies. And unlike our tongue, the pangolin's tongue is rooted down close to the abdomen. To keep their tongue sticky to grab insects, they have an overactive salivary gland which is constantly lubricating their tongue.

Their scales aren't their only defense from attacking ants; their eyelids are incredibly thick, and they can constrict their ears and nostrils to prevent ants and termites from entering.

This is especially helpful since they don't have teeth to protect themselves. Instead, they have muscular stomachs lined with keratinous spines, which they use to break down the prey they swallow live.

They will also swallow small rocks, which, in combination with their unusual stomachs, help mash and grind down the ants and termites in their bellies.

In order to find their meals, which are typically underground, pangolins have huge claws designed for digging. The claws are curved and are perfect for breaking through termite mounds, digging up ants, prying open rocks and reportedly even digging through concrete.

They're also great tools for tree-climbing, though they're supplemented by a prehensile tail which they use for gripping branches when climbing up and down trees.

Other than their scales, our favorite thing about pangolins is the fact that they're bipedal and look hilarious when they walk, kind of like a T-Rex. They do this because their front legs, while adept at digging, aren't as good at walking. They are facultative bipeds, meaning they aren't exclusively bipedal, and spend most of the time on all fours.

Pangolins are solitary animals and will only interact with each other when courting and mating. Males, which are 50 percent heavier than females, won't seek out a female. Instead they will mark their territory with urine or faces, and the female will come to them.

In competition, males will vie for the female's attention by fighting each other using their massive, sharp tails. The mating period usually lasts for three to five days, and their gestation varies by species, from

the shortest, two months for an Indian pangolin, to the longest, one year for the Chinese pangolin, though that number varies depending on which study you read.

Baby ground-dwelling pangolins stay in the burrow for about a month while their scales harden. Then they emerge and ride around on Mom's back and tail, staying with her for about two years, all while learning how to do pangolin things.

Pangolins don't reproduce well in captivity nor do well at anything in captivity to be honest, as they've been described as the hardest animal in the world to raise captive. This is unfortunate because pangolins are the most poached animal in the world. They are sold predominantly for their scales for use in traditional Asian medicine, and their meat is considered a delicacy.

Over a million pangolins have been illegally bought and sold in the last ten years alone, which is almost unbelievable because most people in the West don't even know they exist.

So please, go tell your friends about these awesome creatures, and show them these pictures because pangolins are amazing.

Chapter 41
Tibetan Fox

The Tibetan fox looks like a fox that was drawn by a child. It also looks like a taxidermized fox gone wrong. Maybe that's why it constantly looks like it's annoyed.

Its looks have made it internet-famous for being one of the silliest-looking predators on Earth.

But is there more to this steppe fox than his gigantic square head? There is! But we'll get to that later. For now let's focus on what makes him iconic.

Their faces look like they have been drawn by a kid who's probably never seen a fox before. They have gigantic square faces, tiny triangular ears, a little black circle for a nose, and kinda flat eyes and mouths.

They almost look not real. Seriously, if a Tibetan fox showed up in a *Star Wars* movie I'd call it bad CGI.

But we're not here to dunk on the Tibetan fox all day. There are reasons for all their seemingly mismatched features. Let's give it some context.

Tibetan foxes, as you probably already figured out, live only on the Tibetan Plateau. This vast area of Central Asia is cold year-round due to its extremely high elevation. It's so high and surrounded by such imposing peaks that it's nicknamed the roof of the world.

The Tibetan fox can live at elevations of up to five thousand meters. Mont Blanc, the highest peak in Western Europe, is only 4,800 meters high, so in theory a Tibetan fox could live on top of it with ease.

In general, animals that live in extreme environments end up looking funny. Tibetan foxes are no exception; they just took it to the max.

The biggest reason for their look is their long and dense fur, which protects them from the cold. If you were to shave one or even give it a trim, it wouldn't look too different from a red fox or a corsac fox. They just look like a regular fox that got stung in the face by a bee.

The ears are small and fluffy to prevent them from losing heat, as well as making them less conspicuous to their prey. And their cartoonishly small eyes and nose are adaptations to have the smallest possible amount of skin exposed to the elements.

Their tail is basically a built-in cozy blanket that they cover themselves with when they sleep, just like other cold-weather foxes do.

See! There is an upside to looking like a dollar-store plush toy.

Of course their fur is also perfectly coloured to blend in with the grasses and mosses of the plateau. This is crucial when hunting their favorite prey, the most important animal in the ecosystem, the plateau pika.

The electrifyingly cute pikas are lagomorphs and are more closely related to rabbits than rodents. Pikas are a keystone species because they provide food to almost all the carnivores in the ecosystem.

And by "provide food for carnivores," I don't mean that they go to the grocery store for them.

They also keep the soil healthy by burrowing and recycling nutrients. That is a polite way of saying they eat a lot and poop a lot and, by doing that, they fertilize the soil.

In a typical case of "you are what you eat" the plateau pika also looks like a sketch made from memory. Round body, small ears for a lagomorph, and dirt-coloured fur.

Their huge eyes are always on alert, scanning the land and sky for predators.

Tibetan foxes need all the help they can get to catch them before they dive into their burrow. And so they've been observed following other predators around, like bears, polecats, and birds of prey, who might have caught a glimpse of a pika.

The predators will try to flush the pika out of its burrow, and the Tibetan fox will be there to pounce on it for an easy meal.

But when there aren't other predators around, they'll have to hunt solo or with their mating partner.

Tibetan foxes mate for life and when they have babies they take turns hunting. If one spots a pika, it must get just close enough to pounce.

And when that doesn't work, marmots, hares, and even smaller prey like lizards will do.

Tibetan foxes may not be traditionally cute, or particularly smart, or even great hunters. But they have managed to survive in one of the toughest habitats in the world.

Part of that is because they're great parents and take care of their pups until they're fully independent.

Thankfully, unlike many other fox species, Tibetan fox fur is too coarse for humans to want to wear. And so their main threats are from programs designed to eradicate their primary food source–pikas–from farmland.

Tibetan foxes are not endangered. But, due to their terrain being so inaccessible to humans, and their territories being so vast, we don't know if their numbers are trending up or down. But the research suggests that even though the Tibetan foxes all look super cheesed, it's probably not due to their population crashing.

Chapter 42
Bear Cuscuses

If you've ever thought that you've heard it all before, get ready to be proven wrong. The cuscus is one of the weirdest, rarest, and most fascinating groups of animals in the world that you probably didn't know.

The cuscus is the one animal in the world that made us think the Mandela Effect could be real. How have we gone our whole lives and not learned about the existence of the most wonderfully weird group of marsupials?

Cuscus is the name given to about twenty species in four genera in the family Phalangeridae. They're technically considered possums. Not the North American variety, but the old-world version of them.

There are a few different species of cuscus, and we're going to start with my favorite, the bear cuscus. Don't let the name fool you—they are neither bear nor a North African dish.

They are marsupials from Indonesia, so it makes sense that they have furry bodies like koalas, are roughly the size of tree kangaroos, and share many characteristics with possums.

The bear cuscus is a beautifully strange mashup of many marsupials. They're like a marsupial Megazord.

There are two species in the bear cuscus genus.

Both species are named after the Indonesian islands where they can be found: the Talaud bear cuscus lives on the Talaud Islands, and the Sulawesi bear cuscus lives on Sulawesi Island.

Both animals are extremely elusive, but since Sulawesi is a much larger and more populated place, we know a lot more about the Sulawesi bear cuscus, so that's the one we'll be focusing on.

Bear cuscuses live in tropical rainforests on top of the trees. They have long prehensile tails that lack fur on the bottom and are covered with rough little bumps that help them grip branches. This, combined with their large claws, allows them to climb and jump from branch to branch with ease.

The animal's fur reminded people of a bear, which is where the cuscus got its ursine-inspired name.

Like most marsupials, bear cuscuses are herbivores. They like to eat leaves, flowers, buds, and unripe fruit.

This diet doesn't give them a ton of energy, though, so they're permanently on a low-calorie diet. Because of this, the bear cuscus is slow, lethargic, and sloth-like.

Bear cuscuses move through the trees with such grace that they've also been called "the slow-motion acrobats of the forest."

Bear cuscuses tend to be found in pairs, and they spend most of their time hanging out in trees and eating, living the life.

Like other marsupials, the female Sulawesi bear cuscus gives birth to an underdeveloped baby. She'll have to carry her offspring in her belly pouch for another eight months. That's when the joey will be fully developed and can survive in the outside world.

Moving on to another amazing cuscus species, we have the spotted cuscus, known for their big, round spots. And it's only usually the males that have these spots.

These little marvels are about the size of a housecat and can be found in Northern Australia, New Guinea, and on nearby small islands.

They belong to the genus *Spilocuscus*. Like the bear cuscus, the spotted cuscus is known to be evasive and slow-moving.

Their eyes come in many different vibrant colours, and they have slit pupils, much like a snake's. Since the spotted cuscus is largely nocturnal, these slits are advantageous, as they can handle more diverse lighting conditions–giving them better night vision.

Their diurnal cousins, the bear cuscus, on the other hand, have rounded pupils, which are more suited to lighter conditions.

Then there's the Sulawesi dwarf cuscus, who belongs to the genus *Strigocuscus*. They live on the same island as the Sulawesi bear cuscus, and they also rock those big, bulging, tarsier eyes.

Finally, we have the thirteen different species in the Phalanger genus.

There's the ground cuscus, who lives in burrows they make on the ground.

The northern common cuscus, who's also known as the gray cuscus, has almost-white fur.

Like most marsupials, all of these cuscuses are nocturnal. Except for one. Our buddy the bear cuscus, who's mainly active during the day.

So why aren't bear cuscuses night owls like their cuscus cousins? Maybe it's because they have so few natural predators. They aren't afraid to come out during the day and use the sun to help them find lots of food.

But that's just a theory because, as we said before, there's so much we don't know about the bear cuscus! It's an enigma, wrapped in fur, inside an Indonesian rainforest.

These mysterious animals are only getting rarer, thanks to habitat loss due to deforestation. Poachers also hunt them for their thick fur and meat.

Because of this, Sulawesi bear cuscuses are considered a "vulnerable" species. And their cousins, the Talaud bear cuscuses, are critically endangered.

They may be slow, shy, and perpetually hungry, but we can't help but love these furry little cuscus cuties.

Chapter 43
Prairie Dogs

The prairie dog is the single most important species of the North American prairies. They rule the prairie from the underground, building burrows for other species, fertilizing the land, and barking incessantly at writers and documentary filmmakers.

Despite the name, prairie dogs are not in any way dogs—a fact that becomes immediately clear when you first see one. They are members of the Sciuridae family, and are closely related to the chunky marmots, the adorable chipmunks and my squirrel frenemies who destroy my bird feeder every year.

But unlike your adorable and slightly terrifying neighborhood squirrels, these cuties live underground, in communities called dog towns.

Walk around their colonies and you'll hear the incessant alarm calls of the prairie dog. These calls are part of a highly complex and nuanced language. Prairie dog vocabulary is more advanced than any other animal language that scientists have been able to decode.

Alert calls are a big part of their vocabulary, and while to an untrained ear it all sounds like a dog's chew toy, they can get descriptive, and help them communicate food sources, predator warnings, and social cues.

Their colonies are dotted with holes that they pop out. They are part of a vast underground network of tunnels—some of the biggest dog towns can be as big as 64,000 square kilometers—which is larger than twenty-six of the fifty states.

The massive colonies are made up of family units called coteries. These families usually consist of one breeding male, several females, as well as their pups.

These sister wives will stick together for their entire lives—while the males will leave to seek out new females to mate with every year—typical.

The little families are super tight knit, but they aren't good neighbors—and the males are quite protective about their harem and will bite any trespassers.

There is also a theory that family units will call out to alert a predator to start a jump-yip—what dogs would call a "howl"—and then quickly they'll shut up, so when the predator is closer, it's the other families that are making lots of noise and calling attention to themselves.

The families even have their own language, allowing them to tell kin from strangers.

If you hadn't already guessed given the prairie habitat, black-tailed prairie dogs primarily eat...grass! But they are opportunistic, and will eat insects, roots, sage brush, and cacti, and even larger animals given the chance.

These mega dog towns can be home to as many as 400 million prairie dogs at a time–but since their tunnel networks are so massive, a lot of other species use them for shelter.

If you're walking around a dog town, don't get too close–black-tailed prairie dogs have incredibly painful bites.

You also might run into one of the many species that squat in their tunnels, like rattlesnakes, black widows, and scorpions.

As a keystone species of the prairies, the burrows they dig also serve as homes for all kinds of prairie-dwellers, such as short-horned lizards, burrowing owls, and swift foxes.

These are just a few of the dangers that prairie dogs have to deal with.

With such massive colonies prairie dogs are the number-one source of food for many grassland predators. In fact, prairie dogs support at least 136 other species in the grasslands, which is nice for the 136 other species, but kinda sucks for the prairie dogs. Thanks for taking one for the team, little buddies.

Despite their massive numbers, they only mate once a year in early winter and females only enter estrus for a single hour. One hour, once a year.

She'll have a litter of three to eight pups–and only half of them will survive their first year.

Life for prairie dogs is difficult, and they have to contend with threats from above, below and on land. On any given day, they'll have to dodge attacks from coyotes, hawks, great horned owls, harriers, badgers, and many more predators.

Their two advantages are that they can call out to alert their compatriots of danger and then they can escape through their massive, winding network of tunnels.

However, not every predator is so easily evaded.

Coyotes have been observed teaming up with badgers to hunt prairie dogs. Coyotes are built for speed, but they're too big to

pursue their prey into tunnels. Badgers, on the other hand, are clunky runners, but great at digging.

And so they have formed a mutualistic relationship. The coyote will chase the prairie dogs on land, and when they run into a tunnel, the badger will be waiting inside, having gone in from the other side.

Or, if the prairie dog is already underground, then the badger will charge in to flush it out, where the coyote will be waiting.

It's hard work being a prairie dog.

Because they are such an important prey species, when their numbers take a hit, it releases a wave through their habitat that has a profoundly negative impact on the species that rely on them to survive. It's no surprise that when the population of an animal that provides both food and habitat to so many other creatures declines, the cascading effects can be devastating.

Prairie dog numbers have gone down by 95 percent since Europeans arrived in North America.

Part of this is due to the Bubonic Plague, brought to North America by rats on ships, which decimated prairie dog populations in the 1800s.

Yet the plague persists today, and when it hits a colony, it will wipe it off the map.

The other big impact we've had on them is destroying their habitat to create farmland.

Cattle out-graze prairie dogs and will quickly eat all the food that would otherwise be consumed by the prairie dogs.

As competition for cattle, farmers view them as pests, eradicating them from their natural ranges.

As a result of all of this, the black-footed ferret—which is a species of ferret that has evolved to primarily eat prairie dogs, is endangered. Sadly, there are just not enough prairie dogs to go around anymore.

But there are several ongoing conservation programs, and hopefully soon we will see a resurgence of the prairie dogs and the many endangered animals that rely on them.

Conclusion

Thank you so much for coming with us on this trip to explore some of the most amazing animals in the world. We hope you have enjoyed learning about them as much as we did sharing our love for animals. If you've been watching *Animalogic* from the beginning, you'll know how much we've grown in scope, quality, and purpose, and all of that has been achieved thanks to you and the rest of our audience. Our fans have allowed us to travel the world and amplify our message of nature conservation.

Loving nature is the most effective tool for conservation. People will naturally fight to protect what they love and understand. So if you want to help these animals thrive, tell everyone about them. Tell them why they're amazing and why you care about them. Nature is full of wonders and worth fighting for, but some people don't know that yet. So please join us in sharing this message of nature appreciation and conservation.

Finally, please continue supporting the show. We have amazing projects in the works, which we think anyone who appreciates nature with love. Follow us at youtube.com/animalogic or use this code to go directly to the channel:

Thank you for reading the book and watching our documentaries and for making *Animalogic* what it is today. Catch our next episode next Friday!

See ya!

About Animalogic

Animalogic is a nature documentary series. Founded in 2014, the show has traveled around the world, bringing audiences close to some of the world's strangest and most beautiful creatures. Since then, the series has amassed over two million subscribers on YouTube, 750,000 followers on Snapchat, 40,000 page likes on Facebook, and 20,000 followers on Instagram.

The show was created by Dylan Dubeau and Andrew Strapp, and has been hosted by Danielle Dufault and a growing roster of female science communicators since its inception.

Over four hundred episodes have been released to date, as well as several longform documentaries, and have aired not only digitally but on platforms such as BBC Earth, CuriosityStream and MagellanTV.

Animalogic has blossomed into a network of different nature series. *Floralogic* explores the fascinating world of plants and fungi; *Small Cats Unknown* is an in-depth documentary series on the planet's rarest felines; *World of Birds* scans the sky to showcase the beauty and wonder of the avian world; *Paleologic* is a window into the most fantastic extinct species; and *Second Nature* highlights the most stunning cases of convergent evolution.

These series have won multiple awards, including five Shorty Awards and four Telly Awards.

Mango Publishing, established in 2014, publishes an eclectic list of books by diverse authors—both new and established voices—on topics ranging from business, personal growth, women's empowerment, LGBTQ+ studies, health, and spirituality to history, popular culture, time management, decluttering, lifestyle, mental wellness, aging, and sustainable living. We were named 2019 *and* 2020's #1 fastest growing independent publisher by *Publishers Weekly*. Our success is driven by our main goal, which is to publish high-quality books that will entertain readers as well as make a positive difference in their lives.

Our readers are our most important resource; we value your input, suggestions, and ideas. We'd love to hear from you—after all, we are publishing books for you!

Please stay in touch with us and follow us at:

Facebook: Mango Publishing

Twitter: @MangoPublishing

Instagram: @MangoPublishing

LinkedIn: Mango Publishing

Pinterest: Mango Publishing

Newsletter: mangopublishinggroup.com/newsletter

Join us on Mango's journey to reinvent publishing, one book at a time.